PEOPLE IN THEIR ELEMENT

How to create positive working relationships

Wishing you many more positive relationships.

Yvonne Jan '24

Yvonne Guérineau

Cover image & graphics by: Iron Dragon Design
Book design by: SWATT Books Ltd

Printed in the United Kingdom
First Printing, 2023

ISBN: 978-1-7394020-0-6 (Paperback)
ISBN: 978-1-7394020-1-3 (Hardback)
ISBN: 978-1-7394020-2-0 (eBook)

Yvonne Guérineau
Bournemouth
BH4 8AR

www.yguerineau.com

CONTENTS

PRAISE FOR
PEOPLE IN THEIR ELEMENT

With many thought-provoking questions and ideas to ponder in the complex subject of leadership and working relationships, People In Their Element will serve as a guide for new and experienced leaders for years to come. Drawing the reader to reflect on themselves first is so vitally important, and perhaps uncomfortable, where it is easy to 'blame others' for relationship breakdowns. Then moving onto methods and examples means that the reader has practical approaches to apply, and context in which to do so.

Leadership is no longer about beating people down and out, but about empowering them to thrive individually and as a team. Even if a struggling leader feels they have tried it all, your book and/or coaching will help individuals and teams to achieve what often seems unachievable.

— Elsa Hogan, Fleet and Operations Executive,
Rolls-Royce Defence

There is truly brilliant stuff here, I'm already thinking ahead to how I can implement this with my new and growing team in the new year. Thank you for all the inspiration and brilliant ideas.

— Caroline Waldock, Partner,
Big 4 accountancy firm

Yvonne's book has made me question my role in some of the difficult relationships I've experienced.

We all know it takes two to tango, but sometimes we need someone else to unlock our fixed mindset with a pertinent question or two. From the first chapter to the last I found myself questioning my approach to relationships at work. Now I have a framework to work with that will hopefully lead me to more rewarding interactions with my colleagues.

– Damian Rees, Founder,
makehuman.co

I enjoyed reading it much more than I was expecting to be honest, and it made me do some real self-reflection. I don't read non-fiction/self-help as much as I should – usually prefer to get lost in fiction, but this has motivated me to do more!

– Carrie Collins, Regional HR Manager,
ATC Drivetrain

I loved this book. Relevant, practical and truly thought-provoking in equal measure. Yvonne has a wonderful ability to speak to you directly. It's as if she has written the book specifically for everyone trying to improve their relationships at work.

– Dominic Biles, Head of Organisational Development,
Arqiva

NOTE TO THE READER

This book contains references to childhood trauma although no specific details of any traumatic events are mentioned.

YVONNE GUÉRINEAU

PROLOGUE

For as long as I can remember I've been a people watcher, fascinated by people's behaviour. Despite that, I've always found relationships a bit of a minefield, a cocktail of joy, confusion, and pain. I think even from a young age I understood that complexity intellectually, or at least intuitively, but emotionally I've always found it incredibly difficult to navigate.

Over the years I've invested heavily in my development in this area, partly by design but mostly by necessity, and it's my scars that are now my most powerful allies because it's pain that is often the best teacher. I'm going to share some of my 'teachers' with you and some of my journey.

I know that I'll find this level of vulnerability uncomfortable, but it matters, because there's just no substitute for vulnerability when the goal is connection. So, buckle up and let me tell you my story in the hope that it might serve you in some way.

But where do I begin?

Not all stories start with a big bang and I'm not one of those people with one significant life event that changed my world forever. Some stories, like mine, are the culmination of many events that gradually add up.

I once heard the analogy of a boxer who finally falls to the ground after 100 persistent punches rather than from one knockout blow. That's me. Some of us just keep taking the hits until we get the message!

One of the first hits I consciously remember came when I was about seven. We'd been on a school trip, and it had poured all day. My tendency towards a bit of amateur dramatics started young and when we arrived back, I was embellishing the rain to monsoon-like proportions. My teacher overheard and called me to the front of the class to question why I was bad-mouthing the trip. Of course, that was never my intention. I was mortified and felt completely misunderstood. I've clearly never forgotten that moment of utter humiliation which I am sure set me on the path to becoming a teacher's pet.

I took a few knocks in the friendship arena after that because being the teacher's pet isn't the path to popularity, but despite that, I made friends and loved school, at least until I was 13 when I left for boarding school.

I left behind the international school system where difference was the norm and celebrated, and arrived in a place where the quality of my education and my intelligence was questioned because I'd followed a different curriculum. I attracted unwelcome jokes about my American accent, and managed to upset my peers by misunderstanding and then misusing colloquialisms in my attempts to fit in. There is a significant difference, I discovered, between life on the inside and life on the outside looking in.

I learned what was expected and how to deliver it. I also learned to get by on my own, expecting little and asking for increasingly less support to get the approval that independence attracted. By the time I was doing my A levels I had some very unhealthy eating habits and was on beta blockers for my escalating levels of anxiety.

I think there is only one reason I didn't 'go down' in the boxing ring of my life at that time. The mother of a close friend saw through the fierce independence and refused to let me get away with it, stepping in to take me home one weekend when the words 'I'll be fine' were coming out of my mouth but tears were spilling down my face. She gave me help when I desperately needed it but was trying to refuse it. She knows that I've never forgotten the impact of her kindness that day.

Going off to university felt like being released back into the wild after five years at boarding school. I was desperate to leave but had also become institutionalised. I lacked emotional intelligence and real-world communication skills and was far from streetwise. I was soon going off the rails, skipping tutorials and lectures, and was threatened with removal from my course. It wasn't just the academic staff who disapproved of my approach. I made a habit of picking fights with my housemates until I was finally taken to one side and told that if I didn't change my behaviour, I'd have no friends.

That blow destabilised me enough to carry me to the GP where I cried through my whole appointment and left clutching Prozac, and a promise that in a few weeks' time the darkness would lift, and I'd start to feel better. Unfortunately, the antidepressants fixed nothing, but they did at least take the edge off and helped me to regain my footing in time to graduate with a degree in psychology. I was relieved to be leaving university, knowing I'd burnt a lot of bridges and too embarrassed to try and rebuild them.

After a year of travelling, where my personal life took a couple of hard knocks, I decided to apply for graduate places in human resources, thinking work would put it all right and give me back the structure of the education system, where I would learn the rules, work hard and do well.

I was invited to several assessment centres and did what I thought was expected but got one rejection after another. One of the few companies giving feedback called me a few days after the event to deliver the verdict. They were extremely polite, but essentially told me that the way I'd behaved in the group exercise was not the approach they were looking for. I'd somehow managed to manoeuvre (or was it manipulate?) everyone to agree with me despite steering them towards the wrong answer.

I was still nursing that blow when the business I'd been working in as an interim suggested that I apply for their graduate programme as an internal candidate, and then offered me the job. Because I believed that I'd slipped into the role on luck rather than merit I was extremely nervous when we were asked to complete a personality profile as part of the programme. Should I be more assertive or patient? Was I supposed to be more attention to detail or more communicative? I had no idea how to *pass* the test. My indecision clearly came through in the results because I was asked to redo it.

I partly recognised the person in the description, but that didn't really matter to me; what mattered was that it was a 'good' profile. I'd heard that 70% of senior managers fall into one of four categories and I was in one of those, so it felt like a pass.

My focus now turned to studying for an NVQ in management and completing my human resources (CIPD) qualification. Although no one was unkind, I dreaded the regular reviews because I knew that communication skills would be top of the development list. It was no surprise to me that despite all the energy I was now putting in I was still struggling to meet expectations when it came to interpersonal relationships at work.

My reviews correctly pointed out that I was setting myself extremely high standards and showing oversensitive responses when not getting the reactions I wanted. I felt I had to over-deliver to make up for my perceived faults and deficiencies and it was exhausting. I was still on the antidepressants and every piece of helpful feedback landed like another punch in the face. I was running on empty, and picking myself up became increasingly challenging.

Then one weekend, in search of relaxation, I found myself at a drumming workshop where the sound of the drum was meant to take everyone in the room on a wonderful inner journey. As people described their experiences, I quickly realised that I was the only one in the room who'd seen absolutely nothing. That was the final straw, the harmless little tap that toppled me, and I went down hard.

I spent the next few years working with a very gifted therapist who helped me to make sense of and process the painful memories I'd spent years trying to suppress. The childhood memories that should never have been there. Not all abuse stories, as I came to discover, are stories of fear or aggression. Many, like mine, are stories of people crossing boundaries that should never be crossed, in seemingly loving ways, and leaving behind first confusion and then shame that lingers decades later.

As I worked through my past and saw how my early years had affected every part of my life, I gradually started to see myself and those around me with new eyes. As I began to change on the inside, so did things around me. I relocated, started doing extensive self-development reading, and trained as a coach. I also met personality profiling again, and this time had some of those 'aha' moments I missed out on the first time.

I spent the years that followed on the frontline of people management seeing other people and their behaviour in ever sharper focus and with increasing levels of compassion. I encountered and supported managers on a continuum from weak to wrecking ball and saw a lot of my earlier self in many of the people I met, wondering what pain might be driving their behaviour.

I met bullies and backstabbers, the compassionate and courageous, always asking myself how they came to be this way. I also finally recognised the full power of profiling and trained to use the profiling tool I still use today.

I grew in confidence and discovered that I could now sense emotions around me and read subtle changes in the room when running workshops, knowing intuitively what people needed to hear.

I worked with a coach to fine-tune my use of language, both in my head and with others, and I started to develop the skill of standing back and acknowledging the feelings of others without leaping into the emotional rapids with them. That helped me to reduce the fear of closer connection and made it easier to help others who were looking to fine-tune their behaviours without compromising their identity.

Then came the biggest relationship challenge I will probably ever face. I became a parent. I stopped working for a few years to commit fully to this new relationship and read extensively about child development, where many of the remaining puzzle pieces started to fall into place.

It was then that I realised that my struggle with relationships may have been my biggest challenge, but it had also become my biggest opportunity to make a positive difference to the lives of others.

The idea for a business built on the power of positive working relationships was born.

INTRODUCTION

How would you feel if you found out in five years' time that the person you currently consider a nightmare is actually a truly wonderful human being and that actively avoiding them at work has cost you years of friendship and the business tens of thousands of pounds?

Or imagine heading for the door on your retirement day knowing that your lasting memory of working life will be an endless list of uncomfortable conversations and painful misunderstandings.

We spend the majority of our waking adult hours at work and for far too many people many of those hours are unhappy, or worse unhealthy, because of the relationships they do or don't have with the people they work with.

What a terrible waste!

Would YOU not prefer to spend your working hours enjoying the company of your colleagues and team members?

I have never met anyone who would prefer to be miserable, but I have met plenty who desperately want their working relationships to be the reason they love work rather than hard work. Unfortunately, they have no idea how to get there and have settled for tolerating 'just good enough' or frankly awful, when they could be proactively creating more positive and rewarding working relationships.

You may at this very moment have a burning relationship issue that needs your attention, a tricky employee, or a colleague whose behaviour is driving you to distraction. You may be managing a team where someone is rubbing all the others up the wrong way and your well-placed words of guidance and direction are falling on deaf ears.

Maybe you're supporting a first-time manager or managing your own team for the very first time, doing your best to bring them all together and acutely aware that some individuals are proving considerably harder to relate to and manage than others.

Perhaps you've led teams for decades, and never had problems, and now find that your long-standing signature approach isn't hitting the mark anymore, or at least not with that one somehow resistant team member.

Or maybe, just maybe, you are one of the lucky ones who breezes through the relationship side of management, but you have no idea how to explain to those around you, who want to know the secret of your success, what you do so naturally, and how they could learn to do the same.

This book is for you whether you are an aspiring or existing leader who is facing your first big relationship challenge at work or already actively striving for more positive working relationships and looking to add a string to your bow.

If you are open to shifting your perspective about what might be happening and the role you play in your working relationships, then I can promise you plenty of food for thought and practical tips to take you in the right direction.

If you are hoping for a quick fix or a set of rules to get you and your team from zero to happily ever after in under six weeks, I'm afraid you'll be bitterly disappointed. This is not a comprehensive guide that tells you exactly what to say in any situation to offer you an easy life. The *one-size-fits-all* approach doesn't work well in t-shirts and it doesn't work in relationship building.

I spent 20 years working in a variety of human resources roles, seeing day in and day out how the interactions between colleagues, customers, and suppliers can make or break a team or even an organisation. In all those years advising, training, and coaching leaders, I have never found any one theory, tool, system, or approach that works for absolutely everyone all of the time. And I'm still waiting to meet even one individual who has never faced a relationship challenge and only has picture-perfect working relationships.

I have worked in fast moving consumer goods (FMCG) where the probability of a successful day can change with the weather and in engineering businesses with decades-long contracts and multimillion pound projects. I've been a small cog in a giant 90,000-employee workforce in a shareholder-owned corporation and hands on in the engine room of owner-managed consultancy supporting businesses of all shapes and sizes. Regardless of the context, the same issues have cropped up everywhere I've worked. Same play, different actors!

I have also witnessed time and time again that focusing on the person behind the confusing or problematic behaviour and addressing the quality of the relationships first, before the issues that are troubling people, consistently leads to better and more sustainable results. It's why I don't call what I do team building, but relationship building. Assembling a group of people is a practical activity but encouraging them to care for and connect with each other on a more personal level runs much deeper.

People are complex and unpredictable and how they relate to each other therefore has the potential to deliver a cocktail of experiences and emotions. I've experienced that in my own life, and I've seen it play out in the lives of others. People never cease to amaze me, which is why in this line of work you never stop learning and why sharing that learning over the years has been both incredibly challenging and deeply rewarding. It is also the reason I chose to step away from more generalist human resources work to focus exclusively on relationships and putting people in their element at work. I've come to realise that to create the relationships we truly want and deserve, we need to understand ourselves and others more fully. We need the skills to put people in their element.

To put people in their element, you need to accept that your relationships with others are part science and part mystery. You need to be willing to try and make the seemingly impossible possible. It's a path not without obstacles and challenges, but the reward is the ability to create positive working relationships, which is worth its weight in gold!

I will share with you how I use personality profiling and connection-focused workshops to help my clients, to raise awareness, deepen connections, and build a toolbox of skills to make their interactions with each other at work more satisfying and enjoyable.

It's not necessarily a complex process but that doesn't mean it's easy. You need to consider who you think you are, who others think you are, what others bring out in you, what you bring out in them, and what you witness them bringing out in each other. It's like a giant jigsaw where the pieces keep changing shape. There are infinite possibilities and outcomes for your interactions, and you need to be ready to expect the unexpected, be prepared to reset and try again, and again, and well, yes, again.

What you'll find in these pages is a mix of research and lived experience. I'll share with you what I think and why I think it's worth thinking about, as well as what I do and how I do it. The willingness and commitment to exploring and trying different approaches is then your responsibility. These pages alone will only take you so far.

WHAT TO EXPECT

To help you navigate the information in these pages I've intentionally designed this as a book in three sections.

The layout is designed for you to work through the book from start to finish but I encourage you to see this not as a 'read and run' but as a pick and mix style reference guide to return to and dip in and out of when you find yourself stuck and out of options or as a reminder when you catch yourself falling into a familiar pattern of thinking or doing.

Part One

This section is all about how relationships serve us and why they can have such an enormous impact on our working experience. I'll be inviting you to take a closer look at how communication really works and what might be going on for you and in your team. I challenge you to reflect on your own past, perspective, and circumstances and those of the people you're interacting with and share some insights into how the wonderful workings of your brain (and everyone else's of course) can work against you in your relationships.

Part Two

In Part Two I'll introduce you to the Dynamic Discovery Journey and share with you the unique way in which I guide my clients through a series of steps, taking them and their teams on a personalised journey of discovery from exploring their issues through to infinite possibilities.

A chapter is dedicated to each of these five steps:

1. Issues
2. Investigation
3. Imagination
4. Interaction
5. Infinite possibilities

This section is full of examples and suggestions so that you can set yourself on a path to putting people in their element and getting the best possible results with your teams, so it is important to keep in mind the teams you are responsible for or want to have an impact on as you read.

I will encourage you to ask yourself the same questions I ask myself and to reflect on how I interpret what I find and where it aligns with your current thinking. I will also refer you back to relevant sections in Part One at different times to help pull the pieces together.

Part Three

Then in Part Three you will find a set of case studies. These take you through the Dynamic Discovery Journey again, but this time you'll see how it can be applied to three different teams in three quite different businesses facing very different issues.

You may recognise yourself, one or all of your team members in these case studies, and there may be an uncanny resemblance to a situation you have faced.

This section is designed to be a deep dive and to offer further options for how to interpret what you are seeing and experiencing. There are also additional tips and suggestions that you can extract and apply to your own situation.

THINGS TO PONDER AND TRY

The end of each chapter includes a 'Something to ponder' section which includes a summary of the chapter so that you can easily find your way back as well as something to try or reflect on.

So, now's the time to grab a drink, sink into a comfy seat, and turn your attention to your relationships at work.

PART
ONE

PART ONE

PART TWO

PART THREE

I f you want your working relationships to be part of the reason you enjoy your work rather than just plain hard work, then you are not alone. Relationships are fundamental to being human and to life in general.

In the next four chapters I will be exploring the context of relationships, why they matter, and the impact they can have on our health, happiness, and work performance, as well as why it feels so horribly uncomfortable when they go wrong.

Over the years I have met many leaders and managers who look at relationship skills as just a set of tools, a bit like a hammer, and then question the quality of their 'hammer', or their ability to use it, when they are desperately and unsuccessfully trying to hammer in a screw. When it comes to relationships, trying harder isn't always the answer because relationships are not just a set of processes that you follow, but the result of the events, feelings, and memories that define who you are and how you now relate to those around you.

We'll explore the communication process itself and what might be happening in your interactions, and venture back in time to retrace some of the childhood experiences that helped to shape you and those around you. This has the potential to be emotionally challenging.

I will explain some of the ways that your brain is helping you to make sense of other people and the world at large and where that same functionality throws obstacles in the way of your success.

This section may raise as many questions as it offers you answers but that is part of the learning process, which will also be covered in this section.

Certainly, for me the path to putting people in their element has been a journey of trial, error, and evolution and that is what all relationships are, a journey. We do not always have the luxury of choosing the people we work with, but we do have a choice about how we relate to them.

CHAPTER ONE

THE ROLE OF RELATIONSHIPS AT WORK

PART ONE

PART TWO

PART THREE

CHAPTER ONE: THE ROLE OF RELATIONSHIPS AT WORK

Working life involves other people. There are colleagues and business partners, clients and suppliers, leaders and supporters. Unless you have plans to move deep into the wilderness and live completely alone in harmony with nature, you are going to be interacting with other people. We all exist in relation to and in the company of others and that means that the things you say and do could affect those around you, and how they behave might have a powerful impact on you. The bigger the overlap in your work and the more necessary or frequent your interactions, the bigger your impact on each other could be.

That impact could be life affirming and propel you to the heights of your own potential, or it could be what nightmares are made of. Relationships are a kind of dance. When things are going well it looks beautiful and feels effortless, smooth, synchronised, and elegant. But when things aren't working it looks more like two people tiptoeing in their socks through a room full of pins, terrified of putting a foot wrong, clunky, disconnected, and uncomfortable.

When preparing for this book I gathered the thoughts of other business owners and leaders, interested to understand their views of the impact relationships can have at work. 70% of those surveyed had no trouble describing in detail a working relationship which had affected them so deeply that they were no longer able to do their job to the best of their ability.

There was widespread agreement that tricky interactions had cost people excessive energy and lost sleep, negatively impacting their concentration, motivation, confidence, and even their mental health. There were stories of withdrawing, questioning their own judgement, and holding back in discussions to avoid challenging conversations. This led to important business issues being flagged too late or not at all and unnecessary impact on the quality of their work.

Some shared stories of relationships affecting them so profoundly that they felt the need to leave the organisation and continued to carry the pain of that experience with them for years after the event. Unsurprisingly 65% of people surveyed would rather have an unfulfilling job, working with people they really like, than a job they really like, working with people they don't really get on with. In the perfect world, they would not of course need to choose between the two but be able to have both great work and great relationships to complement each other.

So why do relationships have the power to affect our working lives in such a profound way?

And why does it seem to matter so much to so many of us?

I believe the answer lies in our collective past.

A JOURNEY BACK IN TIME

I believe that the reason we find dysfunctional relationships so painful is because at some level that discomfort is useful. Somewhere in our distant past, evolution selected for us to feel this pain because it served us in some way.

To explain that let's step back in history to a time around 300,000 years ago when the humans of today, Homo sapiens, first evolved as hunter-gatherers.[1] A time when we knew nothing of genetics and modern medicine and evolution favoured the traits and behaviours that best equipped us to survive on this beautiful, but unpredictably quaking and erupting planet. A time when living in small groups and having others around to keep us from harm was the best recipe for survival.

I wasn't around to corroborate it of course but experts appear to agree that around 164,000 years ago we started collecting and cooking shellfish, and then around 90,000 years ago we began to make tools to help with fishing and to generally simplify our lives. Then we began to produce our own food and adapt our surroundings to farm plants and to herd and breed animals approximately 12,000 years ago.

This means that it took us roughly 288,000 years to transition from gathering lunch to farming it and building cities to eat it in. And then the pace of change gathered momentum at a staggering rate so that in the past 200 to 300 years, innovation has included electricity, flight, and trips to the moon. In evolutionary terms we've really only been ordering food to be delivered via the internet for less than the tiniest fraction of the blink of an eye.

I hate to shatter our illusions of evolutionary grandeur but it's not all good news. Despite all of our technological advances to date, and our ongoing commitment to that continued learning trajectory, the human brain hasn't kept up. The organ that makes all that progress possible is still operating with the same systems and processes that were serving us when we were picking those berries and chasing down lunch.

Unlike phones or other technology, as humans we are restricted in our advancement by a vastly slower evolution over multiple generations. And that means that our brain is still wired in the way it was for the world we inhabited 12,000 or even just 2,000 years ago.

The discomfort we feel is evolution's way of alerting us to the dangers of being alone. Before we had health services, safe housing, or technology to feed or defend ourselves on our own, being unable to get on with others could have resulted in going hungry or worse, being cast out from the safety of the group, making us vulnerable to attack. We talk about people pleasing as if it's a modern phenomenon, when in reality, it's probably a prehistoric survival skill.

Of course, it is hard to imagine that dependent and dangerous prehistoric life, when in our lifetime it is perfectly possible to sit at your desk, alone, in your urbanised modern life with limited or no family nearby, whilst being connected to thousands of people via the internet.

This independence which we have come to accept as normal may appear like a sign of progress and even success, but it offers a shallow victory, because as the addiction, stress, and childhood development expert Dr. Gabor Maté beautifully puts it, 'Real connection is between people, not technology'[2].

We can witness this biological driver to seek connection from around the age of six months, as babies become noticeably distressed when their primary caregiver leaves the room.[3] This separation anxiety is the beginning of awareness that survival depends on others, and where children begin to learn how to form and maintain relationships.

We'll come back to the relevance of childhood later, but I do want to share with you here a classic piece of research from the 1950s by Harry Harlow, who isolated rhesus monkeys from their mothers at birth to understand the impact of that separation on the newborn's development.[4] It doesn't make nice reading because the separation had a disturbing impact on the development and wellbeing of the monkeys but the knowledge that it is the comfort, companionship, and love offered by a carer, and not just the food and shelter provided that matters, has had a positive impact on the way we approach professional childcare today.

I appreciate that you are not a rhesus monkey, but that study certainly raised a lot of questions about the role of connection in human relationships and interactions, especially since those monkeys who missed out on that parental connection early on in their lives later struggled to interact with their peers.

Given that those around us at work are no longer small children, you might be forgiven for thinking that the need for connection is no longer relevant, but the research suggests otherwise. Even if early connection needs are met, the evolutionary need for relationships continues into adulthood, although it might not be immediately obvious how. We may not need that connection to meet our basic survival needs the way a baby would, but we will thrive if we can benefit from it.

WHY MAKE RELATIONSHIP A PRIORITY?

You don't need to look far to find research evidence that connection is good for you. It makes you less susceptible to the common cold[5], strengthens your immune system[6], and helps you live longer by as much as 50%[7].

Relationships don't just affect your physical health either, they also impact your mental health. An American study[8] of 4,642 adults aged 25-75 showed that those experiencing what they referred to as social strain, who lacked social support and had poor relationships, were at much greater risk of depression, with the risk of depression doubled for those with the lowest quality of social relationships. That's not easy to ignore. In Johann Hari's book, *Lost Connections – the reason you're depressed and how to find hope*,[9] he very helpfully pulls together extensive research to support the role of relationships in emotional wellbeing.

Physical and mental health are not the only beneficiaries of good relationships. It is now widely accepted that the interactions we have with others at work play a crucial role in our performance at work[10], which is arguably fundamental to the success of a team or business.

Gallup, a world leader in collecting meaningful data about people in business, surveyed 2,708,538 employees[11] across 54 industries globally and found that good working relationships are linked to increased productivity and performance, reduced absenteeism (which makes sense given the link to the common cold), and reduced accidents. People were also less likely to leave the organisation or steal from it!

Relationships have also featured heavily in motivation and performance models for decades. Of those models, Maslow's Hierarchy of Needs triangle[12] is one of the most widely known, probably because it feels intuitively right to many of us that some needs take precedence over others. In his model, love and belonging are the next most fundamental needs to be met once our basic physiological needs for food and water are met and we feel in no immediate danger.

And if you like a good framework, you may be interested in one that is being widely applied as I write, Ryan and Deci's Self-Determination Theory[13]. Their theory puts 'relatedness', which is described as the sense of belonging and connectedness with others, centre stage alongside competence and autonomy, as critically important for our ability to function in society and as individuals in general. There have been hundreds of publications to support Self-Determination Theory since the 1980s so it's well worth a closer look.

If positive relationships really are as relevant in our lives as I believe them to be and research and public opinion suggest, then the natural next step is to take a closer look at what exactly a good working relationship looks like.

WHAT KIND OF RELATIONSHIP?

When I carried out my own survey prior to this book I asked leaders to finish the sentence:

'I know I have a good working relationship with someone if/when...'

How would you answer that?

This question provided a wide range of responses from those surveyed and yet some items turned up consistently in the responses:

1. There is open, honest conversation about things, including the relationship itself.
2. There is trust in each other's positive intentions.
3. Both parties feel heard, seen, and understood.
4. Both parties can be themselves, weaknesses, vulnerabilities, 'warts and all'.

There was an overall sense that it's not all plain sailing, rainbows, and unicorns but that the relationship can withstand challenges and more importantly that both parties can accept challenge from each other, without fear of recrimination or bad feeling. The word 'safe' featured often in the context of offering, requesting, and receiving help as did the words respect, acceptance, and appreciation.

 ACTIVITY

▷ Is this how you would describe the critical relationships in your team?

▷ If you scored the relationships you have with the people you manage or work most closely with out of 10 putting the ones that give you sleepless nights at 0 and those you can't imagine being without at 10, how would they be dispersed along this continuum?

(1) ————————————————————— (10)

▷ Where is most of the mental load for you?

▷ Are you putting more effort into maintaining the relationships at the positive end or do you get sucked into helping yourself and others navigate the unpredictable, choppy, or emotionally shark-infested waters at the other end of the scale?

Perhaps you and your team are hovering around the middle, not miserable but potentially missing out.

Just imagine how different your life could be if you could shuffle all your interactions two notches to the right or if you could ditch anything below 5 altogether.

This is often significantly easier than people realise because the missing piece of the puzzle is awareness of ourselves and others, the willingness and ability to spot and work through misunderstandings, and the decision to shift your perspective.

You may not have had the luxury of choosing the team you manage or the people you work with, in the same way that your team may not have chosen you or each other, but you always have a choice about how you relate to each other. If you are ready to take responsibility for the part you play, believe change is possible and are prepared to invest some time and energy, then big changes are possible.

That might sound obvious but do not underestimate how big a hurdle that readiness can be. We have all seen those individuals who move from job to job and company to company wondering why the same annoying or awkward colleagues and difficult managers appear to turn up wherever they go. I'm not suggesting that bad things don't happen to people, because they do and sometimes moving on is the best solution, but if the pattern is recurring then the missing part of the puzzle might be closer to home.

The celebrated therapist and holocaust survivor Dr Edith Eger writes that 'We do not change until we are ready. Sometimes it's tough circumstance - perhaps a divorce, accident, illness, or death - that forces us to face up to what isn't working and try something else. [..] But readiness doesn't come from the outside, and it can't be rushed or forced. You're ready when you're ready.'[14]

When I was in my twenties, I wasn't ready to hear that my standard approach worked well for some and not for others. When people didn't do what I expected or what I wanted them to do I didn't question my approach, I just thought I had to try harder doing more of the same and getting frustrated with them and with myself. When I was given feedback about how I could adapt, I only heard criticism and rather than adapting my thinking I just worked out how to avoid the feedback. When it finally clicked, that I needed to rethink my thought processes, everything changed. Those aha moments are an essential part of putting people in their element and the Dynamic Discovery Journey, and later in the book you'll see how to initiate them.

IT'S TIME TO CHANGE YOUR MIND

If you are unsure whether you and your team are ready to make relationship a priority, then a good way to find out is by exploring the beliefs that you hold around relationships at work, your relationship mindset. Specifically, you need to know if you have a growth mindset when it comes to relationships.

The concept of growth mindset is attributed to Carol Dweck, whose book *Mindset: Changing the way you think to fulfil your potential*,[15] was first published in 2006 and took the nature versus nurture debate to a whole new level. In her bestselling book she explains in depth how having a growth mindset equates to believing that we have the capacity to change if we want to and learn how to do it.

The interesting thing about mindset is that you can have a growth mindset in some areas but not in others. Until very recently I had a fixed mindset about playing musical instruments. I would say things like 'I'm not musical'. I assumed that it was effortless for those who were 'naturally' gifted. It never occurred to me to ask what those 'natural' musicians did differently, or what I had to do to get there. I saw a closed door and did not attempt to open it because it was out of bounds in my mind. I had to get past that to start piano lessons, and my piano teacher continues to break down some of my mindset barriers in this area.

Whether it's your money mindset, health mindset, or relationship mindset, if you want to make progress you need it to be growth orientated. There is plenty of evidence in the field of neuroscience to support the idea that the brain can adapt and change with time and experience, which means that it's yours for the taking. And you really do need to take it, because if you currently hold the belief that relationship skills are born and not made then you are potentially blocking your own success.

We can quite quickly find out whether you have the most helpful mindset when it comes to your relationships.

 **ACTIVITY**

As instinctively as possible without overthinking, decide if you agree or disagree with these statements:

1. Some people are simply better at relationships than others.
2. Relationships that are meant to be just work.
3. Disagreements can deepen your relationships.
4. If the relationship is hard work, it isn't meant to be.
5. All relationships take effort.
6. When my feelings get hurt, I question if there is something wrong with one of us.
7. When I upset someone, it is an opportunity to learn.
8. People can change if they try.

Items 3, 5, 7 and 8 are growth mindset statements so you score a point for agreeing with any of these.

Statements 1, 2, 4 and 6 are fixed mindset statements, so you deduct a point for agreeing with each of those statements.

How did you get on?

If you tested it on your team, what results would you expect to see?

Rather than asking 'Can I get on with this person?' the growth mindset asks the question 'How can I get on with this person?'; rather than asking 'Can this person change?' the growth mindset asks, 'What do I need to do to get a different response from this person?' If you have a growth mindset, conflicts are opportunities, putting in effort is enjoyable, and when things aren't going your way it just makes you more determined.

THE LEARNING STARTS HERE

Because relationship building is also about skills, mindset alone unfortunately isn't going to get you there. No one ever positively thought their way into an improved manufacturing process or towards increased business performance without taking action. It's like my piano example: deciding that I can play the piano if I want to isn't enough; I still have to learn the notes, and apply myself consistently.

Building relationship knowledge and skills is a learning process like any other, with much to learn, and it may take time to fine-tune your skills. It can be quite a frustrating process too, and there is a risk that you'll give up, so it's important to prepare for some discomfort and understand the stages you may go through along the way and how to keep yourself moving.

One way of mentally preparing yourself for the challenges is by reflecting on the four-step competence model[16]. This model is often applied to skill-building and knowledge acquisition but can work just as well when applied to the context of relationship building.

In this model we start with **unconscious incompetence,** which I prefer to call ignorant bliss, where we are blissfully unaware of all the things we don't know.

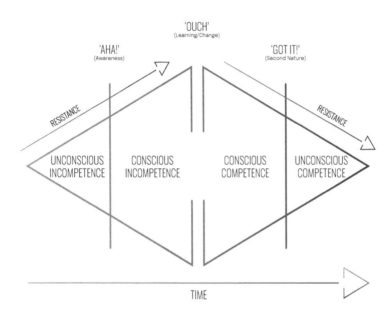

This is the first step in the learning process where we often meet the person who thinks they get on with anyone, even though 50% of their colleagues secretly, or even openly, disagree. We are all here in one way or another. I have always been aware of my tendency to be direct under pressure but until a few years ago I was blissfully ignorant (unconsciously incompetent) when it came to the emotionally loaded vocabulary I was using that was escalating some of the issues I was facing rather than helping to resolve them. Just swapping the phrase, 'I don't think that's important' with 'I don't think that's relevant' was a real game changer.

None of us know where we are unconsciously incompetent (that's why it's so blissful) until we find ourselves in the next stage, which is **conscious incompetence**. This is where the penny drops, and reality strikes. Suddenly it dawns on you that there is room for improvement, and you have work to do. In my example this aha moment came when it was pointed out to me by a coach, but it can just as easily come from a colleague's reaction, this, or any other book, listening to a podcast, watching a film, or attending a workshop. I am now considerably more aware of the power of the vocabulary I use but at this stage I was frequently using vocabulary that sparked the wrong reaction and correcting myself. I am in NO doubt whatsoever that I have many more blind spots still to uncover.

The more you focus on the way you relate to and engage with others the more you will uncover what you didn't know you didn't know. This stage can therefore be a powerful driver, propelling you forward towards more positive interactions. Unfortunately, it can also be a very painful place where you become extremely self-conscious and potentially plagued by frustration. You may find that working through this book highlights things that bring you into conscious incompetence.

If you don't create the right opportunities to learn from your mistakes and are not in the best environment to support your success at this stage, then this is where you are most likely to fold under the strain. It's why I hired a coach to support me with writing this book. I anticipated that conscious incompetence would strike at some stage, and I made sure that I had the support to work through it effectively.

Having a strong ally at work, a coach, a helpful line manager, or someone you trust to talk to are all helpful if you are actively choosing to expand your relationship skills. Anyone you know who is a few steps ahead of you in this area is worth having in your corner.

The process of learning can be painful at times but if you persevere, it leads on to **conscious competence**, or what you could call the comfort zone. When you are at this stage of the learning process you know what to do and how to do it, what works for you and what doesn't, and you can begin to fine-tune your skills, now more aware of your capabilities and limitations. When you first reach this stage you're still at your best after a good night's sleep and on a full stomach, but you are now on track for doing it well or even brilliantly.

In some areas, you may even move into **unconscious competence.** Now you look like a natural! When you reach the dizzy heights of this stage you start to do things without apparent effort or thought, when it just seems to be part of who you are. This stage is where you make it look easy and it feels intuitive. That's when you look like you're a natural at putting people in their element.

TAKING WORK HOME

Before we move on, I just want to comment on non-work relationships. I met my husband at work, and two of my bridesmaids were previous work colleagues. For many of us, the lines between home and work relationships are blurred, or will be at certain times. The pandemic certainly helped to blur those lines even more for large numbers of people.

I ran a poll back in 2020 to ask about the link between work and friendship and 77% of those who responded to the survey had made good friends at work. In my human resources days, I also wrote several policies for businesses around how to manage the complexities of romantic or family relationships at work, so

I'm certainly not the only one who finds people at work to share other areas of their life with. This book is focused on relationships at work, but that doesn't mean you can't apply the concepts at home if it feels relevant, or even just to get some practice and benefit from the positive knock-on effects that work-related learning has at home.

That is part of the magic of investing in your working relationships; the skills are fully transferable, and you shouldn't underestimate the impact your work successes could have in all areas of your life. You take your knowledge and experience with you wherever you go, and no investment you make in adapting your thinking or approach to relationships at work is ever wasted.

SOMETHING TO PONDER

▷ The quality of our working relationships has a significant impact on us at work.

▷ There is an evolutionary logic to feeling discomfort if we are not getting on with those around us, because relationships were, and still are, essential for quality of life.

▷ Research consistently tells us that relationships significantly impact our health, wellbeing, and performance at work.

▷ Not all relationships can or need to be exceptional but taking the right steps can improve them across the board.

▷ The belief that we can create better relationships may mean changing your mindset from 'Can I get on with this person?' to 'How can I get on with this person?'

▷ All learning goes through stages and the four-step competence model can serve as a reminder for what may lie ahead.

TRY THIS

Here are some useful questions to ask yourself before you move on.

If you are managing a team

▷ Who most needs your help with changing their mindset around relationships?
▷ Who is currently living in ignorant bliss (unconsciously incompetent) about their impact on others?

For yourself

▷ If you could only choose two relationships to focus on as you continue through this book, which two people would you choose?
  ▷ I'd suggest you choose one that is likely to be more challenging and one that you expect to be less challenging to give yourself a wider scope to apply your learning.
▷ What would you need to have in place to ensure that you stick with this when things get uncomfortable?

CHAPTER TWO

UNDERSTANDING S.A.F.E.R. COMMUNICATION

PART ONE

PART TWO

PART THREE

nteresting as it might be to know that relationships are part of the human make-up and sit at the very core of our happiness, health, and work performance, you will need to know where to focus your efforts.

To do that we need to start with the basics of how we interact with each other, the process of communication.

We all started to communicate the minute we were born, initially by crying to announce discomfort or hunger then moving on to using more eye contact, facial expression, reaching, smiling, and finally we learned to talk. We haven't stopped communicating since the day we first started, although hopefully most of us have fine-tuned it a little since.

The downside to starting anything so young is that it's tempting to take this intuitive evolutionary process for granted as simple or obvious and to assume that we know how it works or what to do. It's possible that you assume you are in the last stage of the learning process whereas in many areas you may be in blissful ignorance.

To explain what is happening when we communicate, I find it helpful to begin by working through it as a sequence of events. Some of these events are taking place inside us, but a lot of them involve others.

You can break down the communication process into five focus areas using the acronym S.A.F.E.R.

1. The **S** stands for Stimulus.
2. **A** is for Attention.
3. Finding meaning is what we do at **F**.
4. **E** is where Emotions come in.
5. And last but absolutely not least is the **R**esponse element.

Although we generally move through the S.A.F.E.R. acronym in this order, there may be occasions when we skip straight from

Attention to Emotions without Finding meaning, as indicated by the dotted line in the diagram.

This acronym involves oversimplifying what we do to its very bare bones, but it does come in extremely handy when trying to unpick what might be happening and with helping you to decide where to focus your energy.

This chapter will take you through S.A.F.E.R. one area at a time.

 S – STIMULUS

The stimulus is the starting point for any communication. The stimulus is the signal that you pick up with at least one of your senses that acts as a trigger and sets the ball rolling. So you could call it sense too, or trigger, but trigger often has negative connotations.

Because a stimulus is sensory information, it comes in many shapes and sizes depending on which sense was involved.

Most people can happily recite the first five senses:

1. Visual - what you see - such as facial expression or a gesture someone makes.
2. Auditory - what you hear - for example the words people use or the tone in their voice.
3. Olfactory - what you smell - like the fragrance someone wears or the mint on their breath.
4. Gustatory - what you taste - such as the taste or dryness in your mouth when nervous or anxious.

5. Tactile - what you touch or touches you - like the feel of a hand or the brush of a shoulder against yours.

But I'm going to push the boundaries a bit here and suggest that there are actually eight. The other three are less well known, but equally relevant, so just in case these are new to you, here is a very brief overview of what they are.

These senses are:

6. Vestibular - where your body is in space
7. Proprioception/kinaesthesia - your movement and what position you are in
8. Interoception - what is going on inside you

Your vestibular sense, which comes from the information picked up in your inner ear, gives you information about where your head and body are in space, helping you to balance, sit, stand, and walk. Without this sense you would struggle to control your movements and run the risk of tipping over when reaching to shake someone's hand or you'd overshoot and poke them in the stomach.

Proprioception is about awareness of your body's movements and what position you are in. These signals are picked up in your muscles, skin, and joints. Without proprioception you would struggle to control the force you use when patting someone on the back. Sometimes it is referred to as the sixth sense but it might be better described as the hugging sense because amongst other things it tells you about the quality or intensity of the hugs you give and receive.

Interoception tells you what is going on inside of your body, specifically in your organs. This is how you know when you are hungry or thirsty, when your heart rate goes up or you are overheating. This is useful when you need to tell the difference between feeling angry and hangry (hungry-angry) and for identifying and interpreting emotions in general. I think this is both seriously neglected and simultaneously crucial for many of us, but we'll come back to that a little later.

What is so fascinating about how our bodies work is that all eight of your senses can be receiving data at the same time at any given point in time. You might be sitting at your desk typing and see movement in your peripheral vision, pick up the muffled sound of a familiar voice in the corridor and a car on the gravel outside, note the faint smell of coffee in the air, taste toothpaste in your mouth, and feel the seat supporting you. At the same time, you are also receiving input about your core muscles holding you upright (or not), the weight of one leg crossed over the other, and your heart rate slowly returning to normal having just leapt up the stairs to get back to work after collecting that parcel at the door.

You are constantly being stimulated from every direction, inside and out. If you haven't already done it instinctively as you were reading this section, this is your chance to stop right now and do it consciously for a minute.

 ACTIVITY

Tap into all those senses now and notice what you are picking up.

 ▷ What can you see, even out of the corner of your eye without turning your head?
 ▷ What can you smell?
 ▷ What can you hear?
 ▷ What taste do you have in your mouth?

▷ What are you touching with any part of your body and what is touching you (including air)?

▷ What position are you in and where are you exerting pressure or tensing muscles?

▷ What are you noticing about your inner world, your heart rate, and your breathing?

▷ How do you feel?

It is common to use sensory related phrases like 'he caught me on the back foot' or that a conversation left a 'bad taste in my mouth' and yet we often have limited awareness of what we are sensing and how much we favour some senses over others.

The more aware you are of your senses the better you will be at noticing what your *triggers* are (good or bad if you're judging), and with awareness comes the opportunity to influence your attention, which is where we are heading next.

 A – ATTENTION

In theory all senses are created equal, but that's the theory and this is life, and in practice not all sensory data is created equal. We all give priority to some information over other information.

Your brain is designed to filter sensory information and extract what matters and weed out the rest as fast as it arrives. If it didn't, you'd never get anything done, because you'd be so overwhelmed. I'd argue that a large proportion of people are in a constant state of overwhelm because of the excess of information they are exposed to every hour of every day, by choice or otherwise.

Evolution set us up to prioritise some information over other information in the same way that it favours relationships rather than isolation to keep us alive. Although I have no evidence to offer here in support of this claim, I have no doubt that hearing someone shouting in anger is significantly more likely to set your heart racing than hearing a bird chirping, in the same way that a sharp stabbing pain in your leg will generally override the fabric of your shirt gently brushing against your arm.

There are multiple theories available to explain how this filtering system works, and at the time of writing the research in this area is certainly attracting my attention (if you'll excuse the pun). There appears to be a lot of interest in why we find ourselves sucked into our devices, scrolling through social media as if being highjacked by some higher force.

Regardless of the mechanics of how your brain does it, what is relevant to this book is the fact that you definitely do it, and that it pays to be aware of what you are selecting for and filtering out. It is also worth reflecting on the effect that your filtering is having on your relationships.

There are some great examples of what we focus on and filter out. One of them is called the 'cocktail party effect' which is how the cognitive scientist Colin Cherry first explained that you can hear your own name called across a crowded room despite actively listening to the person in front of you, the music blaring in the background, and multiple conversations going on around you.[17] You know your name is important and relevant so you can pick it out against background noise.

That doesn't just work for your name of course, because context and choice can also play a part. If you are deep in thought, a door knock might not be a significant enough sound stimulus to grab your attention, but if you are expecting an important guest, you are more likely to hear the subtle crunch of gravel outside before the door knock even though it normally passes you by.

In the same way that we are more alert to what is in the forefront of our minds, we are also likely to prioritise the signals we associate with impending pleasure or pain because these emotions are closely linked to our past experiences.

Pain is a particularly powerful teacher which is why our language has multiple versions of the phrase, 'Once bitten twice shy'. If you've been burnt once, you're unlikely to put your hand back into the fire, because one glance at it is enough of a reminder to put you on high alert. That's ideal for avoiding fires but can get a bit more problematic when your heart rate doubles every time you hear the approaching voice of the colleague who recently humiliated you in public but is your key stakeholder in a high-profile project.

Luckily, it's not just about negative experiences. Memories that have positive emotional associations also get bumped to the front of the queue when it comes to our attention. You may not have noticed but you are more likely to notice someone in a crowd wearing a t-shirt of your favourite band because it brings back happy memories of gigs gone by.

Your natural filtering systems can be a real lifesaver or throw a spanner in the works when you are trying to navigate your relationships. They allow you to filter out background noise and give someone your undivided attention, but can also draw your attention to just how much the tone in your colleague's voice reminds you of your belittling uncle, or that one word that emotionally transports you back to your worst ever appraisal, deafening you to the rest of the conversation.

The more aware you become of what you are filtering in or out, the more control you will have over getting the results you want in your interactions. It is worth exploring what is going on in you and for you whenever you interact with someone you find easy to deal with versus someone you struggle with.

 ACTIVITY

▷ What is it about what they said, or did, exactly that is affecting you, and in what way?
▷ Are they being rude or arrogant, dismissive or annoying, or is there something they say or do that could be neutral to someone else but is setting off an alert in you?

F – FINDING MEANING

Whatever information your filter is actively bringing to your attention will need to be processed, interpreted, and have meaning assigned to it to guide your response. This is something we do with our thoughts.

We are all running a continual internal monologue (or dialogue in some cases) in our heads throughout the day. Unless these thoughts are linked to a 'big' emotion that stops you dead in your tracks and demands your immediate attention or you are actively choosing to stop and pay attention to them, you may not even notice them happening.

Your thoughts can be positive (YAY, it's finally Monday, I love my work), negative ("*%! here we go again), or neutral (It's 8am on Monday) and they can take many different forms, such as ideas, statements of fact, judgements, questions, or beliefs. They might be specific to a situation, or generalisations. They could involve assessing the realities of the present, imagining the future, or recalling a past event.

And just like stimuli, not all thoughts are created equal.

Your thoughts can support and guide good decisions and motivate you towards positive and life-enhancing action, but they can also be your worst critic and therefore hold you back. The ones that are least likely to serve you in your relationships are those presenting an inaccurate or biased view of the circumstances.

Dunning-Kruger effect

The way we think has been extensively researched and some of the patterns many of us share have attracted names. There is for example something called the 'Dunning-Kruger effect' which describes how we are prone to underestimate our skills in areas where we are excelling and overestimate our skills in areas we need to develop. A relationship example of the Dunning-Kruger effect[18] might be thinking that you are brilliant at reading the emotions of those in your team when you're about average or thinking that you are terrible at showing empathy when you're actually better than you think. Now there's a thought!

 ACTIVITY

> So what do you think you are good at and not so good at when it comes to building and maintaining positive working relationships?
> What evidence is there to support your assessment of your skills?

Confirmation bias

Then there's confirmation bias.[19] This is our natural tendency to find evidence to prove ourselves right. It feels so much better to be right, so we naturally fall into the habit of looking for and noticing things that support what we already believe to be true. If you think you are boring, you can easily spot the three people who yawned in your presentation. The 10 who kept nodding, however, might completely pass you by.

This suggests that if you think someone doesn't like you or that they are going to be hard work, then yes, you'll probably find lots of evidence to support that. You may need to choose to actively disagree with yourself and seek out evidence to prove yourself wrong to break this pattern.

Stereotyping

Stereotyping is another well-known, and potentially unhelpful, thought pattern. Stereotyping is what happens when we put ourselves or others in a mental box and assume that everyone who fits a certain set of characteristics must be the same as everyone else with those characteristics. It has its benefits of course; just consider how much precious time you'd lose trying to work out who to run to for help if you didn't have a box in your head with a set of characteristics associated with the stereotype of an ambulance.

Even though it serves a genuine purpose, stereotyping can lead to unhelpful or even illegal forms of discrimination. If you hear yourself or others using phrases like 'All accountants are…' or 'You know what women are like…' then you are dabbling in stereotypes. You may find that some of them are relatively harmless but that others are standing in the way of great relationships.

Thinking patterns

There are also some very specific thinking patterns that can have an impact on how you behave towards others. There are variations of these, and you may have come across them before. Let's see how many of these you recognise in yourself or in those around you.

All or nothing thinking – This is happening when there is no middle ground; you think someone is either a nice person or they're not! There's no room for a bad day or learning in progress.

Overgeneralising – You're doing this when you write the whole relationship off because someone was late once. Look out for thoughts that start with 'S/he is just someone who… '

Negativity bias – This is where you overemphasise one small negative element of something someone thinks, says, or does. This might involve focusing only on the fact that they questioned one number in your data and ignoring the fact that they contributed more to helping you solve your problem than anyone else.

Mind reading and assumptions – This is happening when you tell yourself that you know what someone else is thinking or what their intentions are without any real evidence to support it. Examples of this might include 'I guess he's just not interested in what I do...' or 'She clearly wants attention'.

Deluding yourself – You are doing this when you tell yourself that something doesn't matter or isn't relevant, or that it is more relevant than it really is. Playing down the fact that you were involved in hurting someone's feelings with thoughts like 'He should have seen that coming really' would fall into this category.

Unspoken rules – Here you are judging others for not living up to standards that you set for them in your own mind, but they probably know nothing about like 'Anyone who eats on a conference call doesn't take their job seriously'.

Emotional skewing – This is when you assign truth to your feelings without the necessary facts. An example might be deciding that someone is criticising you when in fact they just pointed out an error and you feel bad about making the mistake.

 ACTIVITY

> ▷ Hand on heart, did any of these feel particularly relevant to you and the relationships you find challenging?
> ▷ Did any of these remind you of anyone else in your team?
> ▷ Did you do any of them as you were reading?

It is common to find yourself in any of these thinking patterns, but it is not always helpful.

Researchers have found all sorts of things that go on in our minds that you might never have noticed before. Your mind is a wonderful filter, but the filter needs regular cleaning and managing to make sure you get the best out of it.

 # E – EMOTIONS

We now move on to emotions which are collections of physical sensations that we may or may not be consciously aware of.

Emotions appear after thoughts here because that is the traceable sequence of events; you experience something, you think something, and then you feel something. But emotions can also be triggered faster than you can register any kind of thought. You will see this as a dotted line on the S.A.F.E.R. diagram. This is because the emotional part of the brain has the power to override the rational thinking part of the brain, hijacking your attention and overriding your thought process.[20]

I used to well up as soon as I heard an ambulance go by. I had no idea why I had such a big emotional reaction to ambulance sirens until I was told about my brother almost choking to death when I was very small, and an ambulance being called. Now that I know that story it has given me a useful clue to why ambulance sirens override my thoughts and take me straight to an emotion, and I have been able to counteract it. I also know someone who flares up in anger when playfully poked in the ribs. It triggers a bullying memory from their school days. Just the touch sets them off.

CHAPTER TWO: UNDERSTANDING S.A.F.E.R. COMMUNICATION

 ACTIVITY

> ▷ Do you have any examples of sudden bursts of
> emotion like that? Good or bad? Maybe it's a smell,
> a sound, or a tone of voice?

Smell is one of the first senses we fully develop[21] so smells from childhood are often powerful emotion stimuli, and they are particularly worth exploring. Touch isn't far behind.

In the absence of a powerful hijacking of this kind, your emotions are most likely triggered by your own thoughts. You are literally talking yourself into them. You might think that the person 'makes you' sad, angry, happy, or confused, but it is more likely that your thoughts about the person are what is serving you up those emotions.

Being in the presence of or thinking about others can appear to trigger emotions but the person themselves can't do that directly. I have certainly never met anyone with some exceptional superpower that allows them to click into your body and switch on your adrenaline secretion, ramp up your blood pressure, or dilate your pupils. When they allegedly make you angry it isn't really them doing it, it's you.

I have been using the word emotions rather than feelings here because they aren't quite the same thing, even though they are often used interchangeably. It's worth just clarifying the difference. Emotions are the sensations you experience, whereas feelings are the way that you interpret those collections of sensory experiences. We can for example experience butterflies in our stomach and a racing heart on a rollercoaster ride and say we are feeling excited, but if we experience the same sensations before an interview, we say we are feeling nervous.

Emotions and feelings, like thoughts, come in various shapes and sizes, and you can imagine them dispersed along a continuum from subtle to overwhelming. You can feel pleased at one end and ecstatic at the other, unsure or completely baffled, a bit sheepish or completely humiliated, and various other stops in between.

And just to add to the mix, we can also have more than one feeling at the same time. You can be both confused by someone's behaviour and still pleased to see them, terrified that they bring bad news and relieved they aren't weeping.

It used to be common to talk about feelings having no place in the workplace and that showing them demonstrated a lack of professionalism but thankfully we are making big strides forward in this regard. Perhaps whoever started that trend struggled to understand or manage their own feelings.

Emotions are a biological reality and neither good nor bad, they just are. They are neither unprofessional nor inappropriate because they are not optional.

If you 'feel' slightly uneasy at the idea of emotions at work, then it's worth exploring the thought process that is leading you here. It is worth making a note of what that uncovered for you so that you can refer to it when you come to Chapter Four.

Regardless of your current views on the place of emotion at work, emotions or feelings themselves are rarely the problem in a relationship; the problem is often our relationship with them and the need to learn how to express them in a constructive and positive way so that they add to our interactions rather than damaging them. The more aware you and your team are of your emotions, and the better you are at sharing them in a constructive way with each other, the sooner they can serve you rather than holding you back.

Which leads us nicely into the next focus area, the response.

 # R – RESPONSE

Response is often the place where communication training starts and puts most of its focus, because this is where the visible action takes place, where words, tone, and body language play their part in the process.

This is the first opportunity for you to share and for another person to appreciate what might be happening inside you. You could of course offer up a detailed summary of what you are experiencing, thinking, and feeling but generally there is some form of reaction or response to the circumstances in the form of words or behaviour.

Some of your behaviour will be reaction and some will be response.

Reaction

The reaction will include anything you can't easily control like your hands sweating and your eyes twitching or the subtle change in the tone of your voice or nervous pen tapping. Reactions tend to be things that 'leak' out of you without you necessarily realising it.

Response

Your response on the other hand is about conscious choice. It's the words you decide to say or the decision you make to raise your voice or sit yourself down.

Viktor E. Frankl is often attributed as saying that, 'Between stimulus and response there is a space. In that space is our power to choose our response. In our response lies our growth and our freedom.'[22]

Just because responses are conscious doesn't mean they are perfectly executed of course. If you are in conscious incompetence in giving sensitive feedback, then your delivery may not yet match the quality of your intentions.

The way that you react or respond will be affected by a whole range of factors including:

▷ The strength of your feelings and your ability to manage them
▷ Your personality and style preferences
▷ Your core values
▷ The thoughts and beliefs you have around what is, and is not, appropriate
▷ Your relationship with and experience of those around you
▷ The environment you are in, such as an open plan or private office

▷ Your mood in general
▷ The pressure you may be under at work
▷ Your language skills and ability to articulate your thoughts
▷ Your confidence in your own communication skills
▷ Cultural norms
▷ Behavioural habits

However you react or respond, whether you typed and hit send, smiled, shouted, leapt out of your seat, raised one eyebrow, or spoke 10 sentences without taking a breath, once it's done, it's out there and you have no power to take it back.

Assuming another person was in close enough proximity to pick up with their senses any of what you did, your message has been delivered. What you did is now a stimulus for them, and the process repeats itself for them.

You could say that you have now communicated, and your part is done, but you'd be wrong, because your response is only half of the cycle. You now need to wait for the whole process to repeat itself for the other person.

You'll recall how in Chapter One I compared relationships to a dance. Well doing your bit and not waiting around to see what the other person does is like dancing alone. It's a conversational 'hit and run'. For it to be communication with the intention of creating or maintaining a relationship you need to observe and act in equal proportions.

Have you ever noticed what happens when someone gives you their undivided attention? It's not a coincidence that you know it's happening. When someone is creating that sense of connection with you, they are actively watching for how any of their responses land. They are closely watching your expression, picking up on any hesitation, movement, or emotion in your voice. If they have finely tuned this skill then they will know that if they pay attention they can respond to you more effectively, rectify possible misunderstandings before they take root, and even adjust for any distorted thinking they may have triggered in you before it takes hold of the interaction.

ACTIVITY

▷ Is this ability to observe the responses of others an area you need to focus on?
▷ Are there people in your team who would also benefit from this?

COMMUNICATION IN ACTION

I often find that examples are helpful to settle these five S.A.F.E.R. focus areas in someone's mind, so here is the same situation playing out in two very different ways to demonstrate the impact of a change in only one of the five focus areas.

Example 1

An email **(visual stimulus)** comes in from a colleague and you open it. The first line says, 'We've got the auditor in tomorrow.'

Your eyes are drawn immediately to the word auditor. **(attention)**

A trail of thoughts follows. **(finding meaning)** 'Great, not again, we did badly in the last audit. Why didn't he tell me that sooner? We'll never be ready in time; he knows how much springing things on me at the last minute winds me up.'

You are now anxious **(emotions)** about the audit and irritated about the late notice.

You decide to give him a piece of your mind **(response)** and send him a one liner telling him how unacceptable it is that he's dropped this on you at such short notice.

He opens the email and sighs, exasperated, because he only just found out himself and is so sick of being the bad guy who always delivers the bad news and takes the blame.

Example 2

An email **(visual stimulus)** comes in from a colleague and you open it. The first line says, 'We've got the auditor in tomorrow.'

Your eyes are drawn immediately to the word auditor. **(attention)**

A trail of thoughts follows. **(finding meaning)** 'Great, not again, we did badly in the last audit. Why didn't he tell me that sooner, we'll never be ready in time; he knows how much springing things on me at the last minute winds me up.'

You are now anxious **(emotions)** about the audit and irritated about the late notice.

You decide to go back and find out what's going on **(response)** and send him a one liner expressing your irritation and asking for a quick chat to understand why this has come up and what needs to be done.

He opens the email and sighs, relieved that he has a chance to explain it's not his fault, as he's only just found out himself, and he's very happy to help as much as he can.

How different might this sequence have been if the thoughts had been more along the lines of 'Oh no, poor x, I'd hate to be the bringer of bad news like that. I better check he's OK and not drowning in complaints.'

A small tweak in what senses you are aware of, what messages you pay attention to, and the thoughts that follow can have a significant impact downstream on your response.

This scenario might have played out very differently if the message had been delivered face to face rather than via a screen. It's always worth considering the method of delivery, especially for important or potentially emotive messages.

You can't control the response you get from other people, so every interaction and relationship comes with an element of risk. There is a risk that you will be misunderstood, or your efforts won't be appreciated or reciprocated. That is a risk you need to be willing to take. I think it's worth taking, because even if someone isn't willing to put in the effort to meet you halfway, you can still become such a great communicator that you bring out the best in them, and that is a great place to be.

 ACTIVITY

The questions you need to ask yourself now are:

▷ What kind of outcomes and relationships do you want?
▷ How willing are you to start from the beginning, by focusing on the part that you play?
▷ Which of these steps needs your attention?

SOMETHING TO PONDER

▷ There are five focus areas when considering how you currently communicate: Stimulus, Attention, Finding meaning, Emotions, and Response.

▷ Only one of these five areas is about doing anything we'd call communicating.

▷ Senses are vital to understanding the way you interact with others - you need to become a keen observer of the input you are receiving.

▷ We are constantly filtering information and can easily fall into the trap of prioritising information that doesn't serve our relationships.

▷ Thoughts can be your best friend or your worst enemy, so it pays to know which is which.

▷ There is no such thing as bad emotion, but that doesn't stop them feeling uncomfortable.

▷ Your response is never the end of the line; it is where observation begins.

▷ Making small changes even to what you are thinking can have a big impact.

TRY THIS

1. Work your way back through S.A.F.E.R. in reverse. Start with what you did that either went well or could have gone better and then ask yourself:
   ▷ What was I feeling and is there another explanation for that emotional experience?
   ▷ What thoughts came immediately before those emotions?
   ▷ What might have triggered that thought?
   ▷ What was happening in and around me immediately before this event or running up to it?
2. When a colleague or team member shares a situation with you, ask them to elaborate on all five of the S.A.F.E.R. areas to help raise awareness of how they came to be in this situation and how to avoid it or adapt it in future.

CHAPTER THREE

BRINGING YOUR PAST TO WORK

PART ONE

PART TWO

PART THREE

CHAPTER THREE: BRINGING YOUR PAST TO WORK

t's easy to look at communication as a process or system that plays out in a linear fashion from end to end because that's intellectually convenient, but you know as well as I do that people are not that straightforward, and that relationships are an endless stream of surprises, even with people we think we know well.

Despite this complexity we are really all the same, which His Holiness the Dalai Lama expresses so eloquently when he writes:

'We each have a physical structure, a mind, emotions. We are all born the same way and we all die. All of us want happiness and do not want to suffer.'[23]

Whether you find it reassuring or slightly unsettling that you share the same core with everyone around you, it doesn't of course mean that we are all the same person. Our lives are our own unique stories, comprised of millions of tiny moments that have shaped who and how we are today.

It is the sameness, this underlying desire we all share to have a good life, free of suffering, that is core to putting people in their element and why I do what I do, and yet in this chapter I want to focus your attention on difference.

Difference is where the bumps and hurdles often arise in our relationships, whether it's a minor difference of perspective or a much more fundamental difference in values. Difference is what we need to understand, accept, and work with if we want to iron out the kinks that are causing friction in our working relationships.

This chapter isn't light reading, but it is essential reading because it may create new opportunities not only for greater empathy, but also for greater compassion either for yourself or for those around you. Please use this chapter to look at yourself and others in a new light, with new eyes, and with a refreshed curiosity. If you have had a challenging early life, then some of this chapter may be unsettling.

EVERY LIFE TELLS A STORY

Chapter One explored how evolution gives us the explanation for why relationships are critical to our happiness, health, and success and now it's time to turn your attention to your own personal story to consider how your personal past and your unique life experience contribute to your relationships.

People often talk about the events from their past as if they are something long gone, a speck on the horizon, no longer relevant. But this couldn't be further from the truth. The past isn't just a set of events that happened, many years ago; it set the foundations for who you have become by providing the experiences that have wired your brain.

It is now widely accepted that 'neurons that fire together wire together'[24] which is the neuroscientific way of explaining that what you experience with intense emotion, practise, repeat, and/or focus on gets reinforced in your brain and becomes your reality, guiding your experience of the world and your behaviour. That means that those past events are contributing to your everyday activities, written into the map that you are using to navigate your way through the complex maze of relationship building.

Some of your thoughts, reactions, and responses are things you were intentionally taught by caregivers, teachers, neighbours, and friends, but plenty of them came from unplanned, accidental, or even unwelcome events. Chapter Two may have already given you a few good examples of the impact the past is still having on your present thoughts and emotions.

Some of the events that have shaped you were wired into the system so far back that you can't even place where they came from, because they predate your conscious memory; others you may have actively created in response to feedback or to help you achieve a certain result. Regardless of where any of it came from, it's all there, and relevant.

The good news, especially if your past is something you'd like to keep exactly where you left it, is that this map is still being written. Everything you are reading here is either reinforcing the existing links and connections or creating new associations and connections in your brain. Your map of the world and the people in it can be proactively adapted and improved.

But before you can begin to make the changes that have the potential to improve your relationships, you first need to take stock and understand what you are currently doing.

This is not a new concept. The twentieth-century body therapist Moshe Feldenkrais said that 'If you know what you are doing, you can do what you want. If you do not know what you are doing, you cannot do what you want.'[25] With awareness comes the power to understand the present and influence your future.

If you skipped over the activities and reflections in Chapter Two, then I encourage you to go back and have a second look.

 ACTIVITY

Ask yourself:

▷ What am I experiencing, giving my attention to, and thinking?
▷ What emotions am I experiencing?
▷ And how am I currently acting on those?

The devil, as the saying goes, is in the detail! The past may have brought you to the present, but it's the present that is your ticket to influencing the future.

Being able to work with the present is incredibly important because sometimes there are so many complicated and painful twists and turns in the past that we have no desire to dig up and analyse any of it in the presence of our colleagues at work. It is not my place or yours to expect or demand that of anyone.

When the aim is for a team to deepen their connection and develop their relationship skills, rather than beginning with the power of the past it is far easier for all involved to begin with the practicalities of the present, but you are not in a workshop, you are most likely in your own home, or at least in the privacy of your own mind as you read this, so for you, we will begin at the very beginning.

The next few pages touch on childhood trauma and loss and if you feel triggered by anything that you read in this chapter or have a moment of realisation that there is deeper work to do, then please know that help is available and I hope you find the courage, strength, and support to do just that, because it's always worth it.

YOUR FIRST LOVING RELATIONSHIPS

I now invite you to go back to the very beginning, your beginning, to the first relationship you ever had, the one with the person who was there to meet you when you entered the world, your first love.

The first relationship you ever have with your primary caregiver, whether it was your mother, your father, or another adult or child teaches you some important lessons about the role of other people in your life, and what you can expect from them. When children have a need, the instinctive behaviour is to seek out and reach for another human. Those early needs are very simple and there were some basic questions we intuitively needed answers to:

▷ When I cry out in pain, hunger, or fear, does someone come?
▷ Can other human beings around me be relied upon to offer consistent and reassuring support?
▷ Does the presence of other people mean I am safe and comfortable?

For most children (63%) the answer to those questions is yes. They are what attachment theory[26] calls securely attached. These children feel safe in the knowledge that other people, specifically those closest to them, are good for them, that they can expect care when needed, and that it is safe to go out and explore and enjoy the world because there is a safe base to return to.

Unfortunately, the majority doesn't include everyone. Not all children could have answered yes to those questions.

Have you ever worked with a colleague who just wants to go it alone, disinterested in the team, and apparently unwilling or unable to engage beyond the most top-level exchanges? Or perhaps you've noticed how some people seem very eager to please, constantly seeking attention, or desperate for approval? What about those who can't seem to make up their mind, keen one minute to be on best terms with everyone then backing off and even disruptive the next? Maybe you even recognise yourself in one of those descriptions?

There may be all sorts of reasons for that behaviour and one of those includes the possibility that their early relationship lessons fell into the three attachment groups that make up the remaining 37% of the population, the avoidant, anxious, and disorganised groups.

As young children the avoidant group learned that adults were, for whatever reason, not as emotionally responsive as they needed them to be, that their needs were unlikely to be met, that they were held at arm's length or even rejected when scared or crying, and propelled towards independence before they were ready. As children these adults learned to adapt their approach and start to suppress the instinct to seek out help. They learned to rely on themselves.

The anxious group also didn't get the ideal scenario, but they were exposed to an environment where adults were unpredictable, sometimes attentive and nurturing, and other times dismissive, insensitive, or unavailable. Unsure what to expect, these children also adapted, by stepping up their seeking instinct and engaging in constant attention seeking, clinging to their adults to claim and retain their attention.

The final group, the disorganised group, experienced early trauma, abuse, neglect, or in some cases a significant loss, and learned that adults are unpredictable and even scary. To cope with that, they became hypervigilant, controlling, highly anxious, or started to mask their anxiety with power behaviours. They would appear compliant initially and then completely change their behaviour.

Based on these statistics, in any team of eight people at work three could be showing signs of anxious, avoidant, or disorganised attachment.

People thought that Bowlby was a bit radical[27] when he first suggested 80 years or so ago that disturbing or disruptive behaviour in children was linked to their early life experiences, but now there is widespread agreement that what we are exposed to in the first three years of life is fundamental to how the brain develops.

The reason attachment is relevant to our behaviour is because secure attachment has been linked to frontal cortex development, which is the part of the brain often referred to as the 'CEO' area because it's where the higher-level decisions are being made, those requiring reasoning and judgement.[28]

We also know that secure attachment is linked to emotion regulation, because during times of stress when the brain is naturally flooded with stress hormones, it is the soothing behaviour of a caregiver that reduces stress hormones in the young brain and allows self-regulation pathways to map. It's our attachment relationship that first taught us how to soothe ourselves under pressure.

At the extreme end of the scale, children with trauma in their early lives are more likely to struggle with regulating their feelings, have challenges in their social relationships, aggression, low self-esteem, and depression.[29]

This might at first glance seem unrelated to the workplace, but those early connections are extremely powerful and will still be impacting working relationships much further downstream unless effort is put into changing them. The percentages quoted for children above are replicated in the adult population, which means the similar proportions of avoidant, anxious, or disorganised attachment styles are likely to be showing up in teams in the workplace.

If you have someone in the team who consistently struggles with self-esteem, is insecure about their own worth, easily takes the blame, or needs a lot of reassurance that they are good at their job, then they may have anxious attachment.

If you work with someone who seems happy with who they are, sociable with good self-esteem, but who keeps people at arm's length, avoiding real closeness or intimacy and never moving beyond surface level social interactions, then they might be avoidant.

Disorganised attachment might show up as mixed messages, wanting to belong but concerned about trusting others, or being rejected. If you are seeing self-sabotage, then this may be at play. It's tough when you want connection but expect disappointment.

As attachment style is not something that comes up in everyday conversation and people may not even know what their style is, it may not be possible to manage directly. Leaders need to be aware of the needs of their team and just having some awareness of attachment may give you some powerful clues to what might be needed, and more often than not that need is consistency.

Consistency is relevant for everyone to some degree even if securely attached as it helps with building trust, but inconsistency may have a more extreme impact on those not securely attached. Someone who is anxiously attached, for example, may become more prone to attention seeking, whilst someone with an avoidant attachment may just write you off as a poor leader and disengage.

If you are interested in finding out your own attachment style, then The Attachment Project has a quiz[30] you can take. I knew my attachment style before taking the quiz and the result was accurate.

If you had or have a challenging relationship with your parents or early caregivers, then this may make uncomfortable reading so please take that into account before taking the quiz.

CHILDHOOD EXPERIENCES

Childhood is not of course just about those first few years of life; we are exposed to plenty of life experiences before we become adults. Hopefully plenty of fun times, happy memories, and positive learning experiences which give us strong foundations for adult life.

For a larger proportion of the population than you may imagine, however, these early years also include challenging times and traumatic events, collectively known as adverse childhood experiences or ACEs, which the Centers for Disease Control and Prevention[31] have defined as 'potentially traumatic events that occur in childhood (0-17 years)'[32].

Dr. Felitti is associated with identifying a link between childhood trauma and unhealthy coping mechanisms in adults and then a ground-breaking study (which he led) by the Centers for Disease

Control and the Kaiser Permanente health care organisation in the late 90s provided strong evidence to support that.[33]

ACEs are split into three broad categories:

1. Abuse
   ▷ Emotional abuse
   ▷ Physical abuse
   ▷ Sexual abuse
2. Household challenges
   ▷ Mother treated violently
   ▷ Substance abuse in the household
   ▷ Mental illness in the household
   ▷ Parental separation or divorce
   ▷ Incarcerated household member
3. Neglect
   ▷ Emotional neglect
   ▷ Physical neglect

A study carried out in the United Kingdom more recently, in 2014,[34] found that 47% of people had experienced at least one ACE, with nine percent of the population having four or more in their past.

The bulk of the research on this subject is linked to the impact this can have on health rather than relationships, but I know from my own experience that health impacts relationships, so I have chosen to include it here because the effects of ACEs have the potential to show up in team dynamics or in a working relationship in the same way that attachment style can. In fact, they may well be the reasons for a specific attachment style.

In my experience some of these topics are more likely to be considered mainstream topics of conversation at work than others. Having divorced or separated parents, or an early bereavement for example, may be mentioned as teams share how they tend to spend their holidays, whereas experiencing abuse probably won't.

It is also relevant that events may not be remembered by someone as traumatic depending on the circumstances of those events, the details they recall, or how it was interpreted by them at the time. Someone may well look at this list, see more than one item that applies, and tell themselves that it wasn't that bad, or that others had it worse.

Regardless of how events have been interpreted, which we will come back to again in the next chapter, they are likely to have contributed in some form to the emotional responses and thinking patterns you uncovered in Chapter Two. ACES are likely to have an impact on the way you see the world, your perspective, beliefs and thought processes and, yes, therefore also on your interpersonal relationships.[35]

The important thing to bear in mind here is that not all those with a challenging past are or look as if they are struggling. There are many successful business owners and senior leaders who seek support to improve the communication and dynamics in their teams and only then start to connect the dots between their past and the way they are feeling about and tackling certain issues in their team.

Several of my clients have started or returned to therapy of some kind because of uncovering these associations and realising that the unconscious coping strategies that served them in their childhood are now an obstacle to progress.

When stories of this nature rise to the surface for a leader directly or for someone within their team my advice is always to seek further professional support or encourage the other person to do so. I am not shy of actively encouraging that. I spent years running away from my early trauma and I can say with certainty that that approach doesn't work. It's a bit like playing hide and seek with your memories, asking them to hide and then pretending you're not playing anymore. At some point the memories will get restless, resurface, and come looking for you.

You don't need to go through life assuming that behind every miscommunication or misunderstanding lurks a hidden trauma, but the statistics suggest it's a real possibility that in most teams there will be at least a few ACEs between you. It's important to keep an open mind to the possibility.

SOMETHING TO PONDER

▷ At our core we all want to be happy, but on the surface, we are all different in our approach to achieving it.

▷ We never leave the past behind us; we integrate it into who we are, how we think, and what we do, so you can't ignore it, you need to work with it.

▷ This work has the potential to be therapeutic, but it is not a replacement for therapy. If there is deeper work for you to do it is important to do it.

▷ The role adults play in our early lives can affect our attachment and continue to affect our behaviour towards other adults at work.

▷ 47% of people had experienced at least one adverse childhood event that might be affecting their interactions with others, with nine percent of the population having experienced four or more.

TRY THIS

▷ How much do you know about the early lives of the people in your team?

    ▷ Did they have a happy childhood?

    ▷ How do they relate to their family?

    ▷ Who was their greatest cheerleader in their early life?

    ▷ Who do they turn to in times of need?

    ▷ What topics do they shy away from?

    ▷ What do they talk about as their early success?

▷ Do you know the impact of your past on your life? If you had to answer the same questions for yourself,

    ▷ which would be the most difficult to answer, or most emotionally challenging?

    ▷ what are you not comfortable sharing? Why not?

    ▷ how has it shaped the way you behave around others at work?

CHAPTER FOUR

WHAT'S ON YOUR MIND

PART ONE

PART TWO

PART THREE

CHAPTER FOUR: WHAT'S ON YOUR MIND

When I was studying psychology as an undergraduate, I was often asked if I knew what people were thinking. There is, or at least there was at that time, a common misconception that knowledge of psychology means you can read other people's minds and predict behaviour.

That would be incredibly useful, if perhaps a bit dull after a while, but it's not true of course. Psychology unfortunately doesn't go that far just yet, but it has started to explain underlying and generalised principles of how the brain works and how that might impact our relationships, which is a huge help for those of us who want to be proactive in this area.

There are a multitude of behaviours that we appear to share with others regardless of our personal life story as well as similar patterns (or traps) we are all at risk of falling into. Knowing about them won't help you predict someone's every move, but awareness of their existence does give you the edge if you want to seize every opportunity to be more intentional in your interactions, and the quality of your relationships.

This chapter is all about the way our minds organise the world.

HOW THE MIND WORKS

As people we are constantly making relationship decisions, from choosing who to sit next to in a meeting, to telling a colleague what we REALLY think. Because of all the factors covered in Chapter Two and Three, you, and those around you, make all these decisions in the face of uncertainty. You have to, because you can never fully predict what the outcome or consequences of your actions will be.

You have no choice but to accept a certain level of uncertainty because you can't possibly call for a 20-minute timeout to consider multiple options every time you encounter a simple social situation; it's just too slow. So, instead of starting from scratch our brain has evolved to refer to existing patterns of thinking and models of the world. The developmental psychologist Jean Piaget coined the term 'schemas' to describe these mental frameworks or models that we use to organise our world.[36] Think of them as mental filing systems, that you slot new information into when it comes your way.

Just for a moment, imagine being little again and seeing a cat for the first time. You call it a dog; after all, it is a living, moving, four-legged furry thing, and in your family one of those is called 'the dog'. But someone corrects you and explains that this four-legged furry animal is a cat. Now the animal section of your filing system needs to reorganise and expand. You create a new category called cat to add to the animal section next to dog. Both are four-legged and furry but one meowing with sharp claws, and the other woofing and tail wagging.

You may never have given any thought to how you know a cat is a cat and not a dog because these models start to form from a very young age and are also stable over time, so stable in fact that I know someone who refers to fluffy miniature dogs as toilet brushes! He loves dogs, but something smaller than a cat clearly fits more comfortably into his model of bathroom appliances than into his dog model.

It's important to differentiate between a schema and a belief because you don't see a dog and *believe* it's a dog; you see the component parts and automatically put four legs, a bark, and various other characteristics together to conclude it's a 'dog'. It's more like pattern recognition. Beliefs are the bedfellows of schemas because our models of things often come hand in hand with beliefs, but schemas are much harder to shift, because they are the structure or skeleton to which the beliefs are attached.

You have schemas for social situations and people, including yourself and not just for animals, minerals, or vegetables. Without perhaps realising it, you have a schema that sets your expectations about the role of a receptionist, how interviews work, what makes a good friend, leader, or colleague and how to behave at the works party.

Whatever information and emotion you've encountered in your life and how you filed it, is unique to you and you potentially have a very different set of models to those of others around you. As already covered in the last chapter, early experiences can have a big impact on your filing system, but so can later experiences which you continue to encounter as you add to and evolve your filing system.

Eating out is a great example of how a schema might attract your attention. If you have only ever eaten out at fast-food restaurants with family or friends in your early life, the first time you are invited to a silver service restaurant for work you might suddenly be flooded with new information that just doesn't fit into your 'eating out' schema. This might include being escorted to a seat, engaging with a wine waiter, managing several sets of cutlery, and how to tip. Previously totally at ease when eating out, you now have no rules about what is expected or what patterns to follow and need to put considerably more mental effort into deciding what to do.

When these models are serving you well, they act like a behavioural fast track system, speeding you along with no real thought required; you just pull out the file, and follow the pattern. The models cease to serve you so well when they block creative thought and make you rigid in your approach.

Schemas often have their roots in various biases and thinking patterns, which were covered in Chapter Two. Schemas can influence our attention, with a tendency for us to notice and accept what fits (remember confirmation bias) and a tendency to explain away or reject the things that don't fit (like the toilet brush).

When I was growing up, I had a tattoo schema that said that you only find tattoos on the uneducated, sailors and convicts, and that those displaying them are best avoided. I wasn't alone in this because a schema can be cultural and generational. As I write, discussion of the 'appropriateness' of tattoos is a hot topic on social media because old schemas can be hard to shift. This is especially the case if a schema was created with a strong emotion like fear or disgust attached to it as was the case for me. If tattoos spell danger or social exclusion you wouldn't instinctively go looking for them and choose actively to engage with people displaying them until there is a compelling need or reason to do so.

In my early twenties, if I met someone with a tattoo, I immediately felt uncomfortable. It wasn't that I was judging the person as such, it was just a completely automated response, tattoo sighted, file open, suspicion engaged. Now in hindsight, it's almost comical, but back then, it was a matter of self-preservation.

You probably have similar examples of your own and you may not even know that you have some of them until you are challenged on them, someone falls foul of one, or demands that you rethink your position. 'Men don't show feelings' and 'Women belong in the kitchen' ring any bells?

 ACTIVITY

What if your model of what makes a good colleague differs from the models of the people you work with, but you never discuss it? How does that affect how you interact with each other?

▷ What are the unspoken rules you work to?
▷ Are there situations that you respond to in certain ways but have never asked yourself why?

Maybe you hold back sharing personal information at work because you have a work schema that includes 'Work and friends don't mix' after being badly hurt when a colleague blurted out something you thought you'd shared in confidence at a social event. That particular rule has a priority position in your filing system because of the pain associated with it. (Remember that neurons that fire together, wire together.)

▷ Can you bring to mind any examples like this?

If you are hesitating, resisting, or quick to jump to conclusions in certain situations then an underlying schema may be the culprit, and it is worth starting to unpick it and working out if it's serving you and your relationships. Even a toilet brush can be someone's best friend!

It's neither easy nor comfortable to override an established schema, so it requires some investment of energy, and you may need to be gentle and supportive of yourself and those around you when this is proving challenging. Moving from blissful ignorance to realisation when it comes to our models of the world is no different than realising how consciously incompetent a driver we are when we first learn to drive after years of formula one level backseat driving.

If you are struggling to be compassionate here, then now is a good time to revisit the 'It's time to change your mind' section of Chapter One or to ask yourself whether you could do with more of a growth mindset.

Given that schemas are self-reinforcing, a lot of what I do in my work is about raising awareness that they exist, so that people can make a conscious decision to become receptive to and even seek out new information to re-evaluate them. Sometimes just a little tweak is all it takes to turn a tricky relationship into a future friendship.

OH LOOK... A SHORTCUT!

Alongside schemas we also have rules of thumb, or shortcuts, called heuristics that we use to help speed up our decision-making.

In Chapter Two I introduced you to the Dunning-Kruger effect which describes how we under and overestimate our skills, and confirmation bias, where we focus on something and find more and more evidence to prove ourselves right, and there are plenty more where those came from.

You don't need to know them all or what they're called, but I'm going to share a few more to give you deeper insight into where you might inadvertently be getting in your own way in your relationships.

As you read through this section you may notice that there is more method and process at play in your relationships than you realised, and where there is method there are opportunities for process improvement.

Representativeness

We'll begin with our tendency to predict that something is likely to happen because we've seen something similar before. The psychologists Kahneman and Tversky (1974) called this 'representativeness'.[37]

In their work they give the example of a man called Steve who is either a farmer, salesman, airline pilot, librarian, or physician.

They describe Steve as '... very shy and withdrawn, invariably helpful, but with little interest in people, or in the world of reality. A meek and tidy soul, he has a need for order and structure, and a passion for detail'.

Based on that description, do you think he is a farmer, salesman, airline pilot, librarian, or physician?

Chances are you said librarian. Why? Because the description of Steve is like the stereotype of the librarian. Statistically and with demographics and numbers of libraries considered, it's more likely he's not a librarian, but who needs facts when we think the answer is obvious!

Just consider for a moment how quickly you may have jumped to conclusions about someone in your team in this way. You may not have had them down as a librarian, but you may have decided that they must be a stickler for detail because they studied mathematics, an assertive driver because they drive a BMW, or have a messy house because they have young children. It is easily done, and often a useful shortcut, until you find you've got completely the wrong end of the stick.

I encourage you, like I do all my clients, to go back and check how many of your 'facts' are genuine facts and how many have come from this representativeness trap. Think of it as 'taking the person back out of the box you've put them in and having a look at them with fresh eyes'. It's not hard to do; just ask them something you think you know the answer to and see what you get back.

Anchoring

Next up is a cognitive bias called 'anchoring'. This involves us relying too heavily on the first piece of information offered to us and then using it as the foundation or reference point for later information.

A good example of this is in sales negotiations where the anchor is the first price that you are offered by a salesperson; in relationships this might be the first thing you witness, are told about someone, or they share about themselves. Rather than logically assessing every piece of information that comes afterwards, that first piece of information acts as an anchor to evaluate what comes next.

If for example you first meet someone at a project briefing where they are remarkably outspoken about their objections to key issues, this is now your reference point for this person, their 'normal'. If, when you next meet them, they are less objectionable you are more likely to assume that they are still objectionable but have been asked to back off a bit, are making more of an effort to hold back, or have lost interest in the project.

We often hear about the need to make a good first impression, and I agree to some extent, but not everyone is good at 'first impression management' so you can give it significantly more credit than it deserves. If you want to create better relationships, you need to make looking beyond the first impressions a habit. That first impression is just the tip of the relationship iceberg, and you don't want the relationship to go down like the Titanic because you didn't take the time to look twice.

Better than average

If you are of above average intelligence, you can probably recover from those iceberg situations quite quickly, give people a second chance, and not jump to too many conclusions too quickly. But the question is, are you above average intelligence?

Yes, it's a trick question.

If you would put yourself into the above average category, then you are one of 70% of men and 60% of women who do[38]. Of course, that's mathematically a bit problematic, as only half of us can be above average otherwise it isn't the average.

This 'better than average effect' is a measurable effect and can also cause you trouble in your relationships. If for example you apply this effect to your communication skills and conclude that you are above average at giving feedback, then you may miss opportunities to develop in this area. Whilst it's great for keeping you optimistic, it may leave your teammates or direct reports wondering why you are less open to, or worse, resistant to working on the areas where they'd mark you down as 'could do better'.

Communication is a broad topic and it's worth taking a closer look and even getting some wider feedback to check where you might be applying the 'better than average' effect to your relationship skills.

Halos and horns

That's not all yet. Have you ever noticed how the top performer in some businesses or teams can't seem to put a foot wrong? Amazing as they might be, you may also have fallen victim to the 'halo effect'.

This bias is all about letting our positive opinion of someone influence our assessment of them in other situations. Imagine that top performer wearing a halo, like an angel. Well, angels don't make mistakes or bad decisions and they would certainly never upset someone. If something has gone wrong, then the other person must have been feeling a bit oversensitive or be missing something. That halo appears to cancel out objectivity which can cause tensions or worse, unfair treatment in teams.

A close relative of the 'halo effect' is the 'horn effect', and yes you guessed it, it's about assuming that the person who messed up the last presentation probably messed up this one too (well, it must be, because 'halo' would never have done that!). We saw those devilish horns once, so we expect to see them again.

If you've not already done this as you were reading, I recommend just taking a moment to reflect now.

> ▷ When is the last time two people you know did something you found annoying or unhelpful and for one of them you thought, 'I KNOW he is a lovely person, he's only human and having a bad day' and for the other you thought 'Typical, what did I expect?'

Is it possible that they were both having a bad day but you're more likely to give one leeway than the other? Objectivity isn't always easy when we have halos and horns attached to people, so it may be helpful to enlist some help with this.

Fundamental attribution error

I'll finish this section with just one more bias, the 'fundamental attribution error'. This one is particularly important, so I hope you're sitting comfortably. According to this bias, when we are making judgements about people's behaviour, we believe that their actions are more likely to be the result of their personality rather than other factors, like the environment over which they may have absolutely no control.[39]

I'll just repeat that to let it sink in.

When someone does something, you are more likely to assume that it's who they are, rather than the result of the circumstances they find themselves in.

Interestingly though, when it happens to you, you are much quicker to blame the circumstances.

What that means is that when you are late it's because you are under a huge amount of pressure with a tight deadline looming and had 30 emails that needed a reply before you could get here. When your colleague is late however it is probably because she's a bit disorganised. Never mind that she has the same types of deadlines and a similar number of emails to wade through. That's fundamental attribution error.

When it's you, you know all the context affecting you and take it into account, whereas when it's someone else, it's a lot faster and easier to assume it's just them. As you can imagine, conflicts can quickly escalate when we expect others to be total masters of their environment even though this is completely unrealistic.

There is also a flip side to this bias, the fact that we are more likely to take credit for our successes and put our colleagues' success down to circumstances. In evolutionary terms I imagine this is a marriage of convenience between saving time and feeling good about ourselves. It might however be better for your relationships if you gave others more credit for their successes and took more of an interest in the circumstances surrounding their failures.

BIAS MANAGEMENT

When it comes to all of these biases, awareness is your ticket out of the trap, and you may want to keep some questions handy for when you catch yourself either making others the masters of the universe or writing their successes off to circumstance.

Here are some you could try:

▷ What am I missing here that may have affected what they did?
▷ What barriers are they facing?
▷ Could this be a system or process issue?

$\triangleright$ What other reasons might there be for them doing that?
$\triangleright$ What would have happened to me to respond like that?

THAT'S JUST MY PERSONALITY

We've already touched on personality above and how readily we assume that personality is the main driver of behaviour. Now let's dig a bit deeper into this topic.

Differences in personality are accessible to anyone, whether they are only looking for simple communication tips and suggestions or ready to do some deeper reflection about how to get on better with others. It is undoubtedly one of the fastest, and least threatening, ways to start people on a journey of self-awareness and relationship building, because it's something we can all relate to regardless of our life history or our willingness to share that with others. It has also fascinated us for hundreds of years, and therefore has a much longer history than many of the psychological findings that you have seen up to this point.

The idea that we have different personalities dates as far back as the ancient Greek philosophers who tried to explain some of the patterns that we see in human nature using four temperaments: choleric, melancholic, sanguine, and phlegmatic.

Then in 1921 the Swiss psychiatrist and psychoanalyst Carl Jung published his thoughts on psychological types[40] and described in intricate detail how our preferences affect the way we see and interpret the world. Jung, like the ancient philosophers, believed that there are clear patterns in the way people show up and yet he also believed that we are all unique and an exception to the rule.

Jung's approach to honouring both our uniqueness and our similarities is no doubt the main reason that his work has stood the test of time and continues to underpin many personality profiles today, including the well-known Myers-Briggs Type Indicator® (MBTI®) assessment and Insights Discovery®.

Jung was interested in how we relate to the world around us and explained our differences as lying along three scales. He called one scale attitude, which extends along a continuum from extraversion to introversion. The other two scales contained what he referred to as the four functions: thinking, feeling, sensation, and intuition.

Extraversion and introversion are terms which now turn up in everyday conversation but are often misinterpreted. People often confuse introversion with shyness and extraversion with confidence when that's not quite what Jung had in mind. He was describing the way in which we prefer to engage with the world around us, whether we are more internally focused and reflective (introversion) or externally focused towards engaging and taking action (extraversion).

Jung's functions were about our approach to decision-making and the way we process information, whether we are more likely to lean towards a more logical (thinking) approach or show a preference for evaluating based on value judgements (feeling), whether we lead with our senses and evidence (sensation) or prefer to make inferences about the possibilities (intuition).

The research into personality is ongoing, with a wide variety of theories and tools now available to help explain how personalities differ and show up in our behaviour, and they are certainly not all based on Carl Jung, but I confess a preference for the work of Jung and his attitudes and functions.

The profile I currently use has Jungian roots and is like 'colour by number' for understanding human behaviour, because it uses exactly that, colour, to explain personality differences by translating Jung's *attitudes* into colours, each of which is associated with a set of needs, wants, fears, and of course behaviours.

This colourful approach certainly makes it memorable, but what matters most is that the information given in any report is not just accurate but validating for the person receiving it. Everyone wants to feel seen, heard, and understood, and the right tool, used in the right way, will do that. It certainly makes your life easier if it is written using non-judgemental and supportive language.

What is important to keep in mind is that there is no good or bad end of the scale or continuum, there are just two very different extremes when it comes to how we might approach doing the same things; often the same intentions are just packaged in different ways.

Regardless of whether you are at the extreme end of extraversion or introversion, for example, you have the same potential to have a good or a bad day. The engaging and dynamic extravert can overflow into becoming melodramatic whilst the considered and considerate introvert can overflow into being distant.

When working with personality, whether you use profiles or just reflect on different styles, you can quickly see what you have in common with those around you and where you differ, creating a common language that allows you to talk about a style or an approach without attaching a judgement to it.

Given that misunderstandings are often a major cause of difficulty in working relationships, it can be truly liberating to see in one easy glance why this might be happening and where to find common ground using personality preferences, whichever way the tool you choose presents them.

This brings me full circle to where I began this book, on the fundamental need we all have, to be seen, heard, and understood and to feel, or better still KNOW, that we belong and can create meaningful connections to others.

We've covered a lot of ground in Part One and there has been plenty to reflect on. Now in Part Two I am going to show you how to put all these pieces together the way I do with my clients, so that you can begin to do the same in your own team.

SOMETHING TO PONDER

▷ Understanding some of the principles of how the brain works can be extremely helpful for making your relationship building more intentional.

▷ We all have mental models to organise our world, a bit like information filing systems so that we know a dog is a dog and not a cat without any apparent effort.

▷ Depending on what information and emotion you've encountered in your life and how you filed it, you may have a very different set of models to those around you.

▷ Heuristics are shortcuts we use to make decisions including:

  ▷ Representativeness - predicting based on past experience.

  ▷ Anchoring - relying too heavily on the first piece of information offered to you.

  ▷ Better than average effect - assuming that you are above average.

  ▷ Halo and horn effects - where existing positive or negative impressions of people influence our feelings about them in future situations.

  ▷ Fundamental attribution error - believing someone's actions are more likely to be the result of their personality rather than other factors out of their control.

▷ Personality is often the most accessible introduction to relationship building at work.

▷ If used wisely, personality profiling works like a kind of 'colour by number' for understanding human behaviour.

TRY THIS

For profiling tools to be accredited they need to demonstrate reliability (does it offer consistent results over time) and validity (does it measure what it says it measures).

You can apply the same tests to your mental models and decisions.

Example: 'the best meetings always start and end on time'

▷ Reliability
  ▷ Does this apply to all types of meetings?
  ▷ With anyone?
  ▷ Regardless of the topic or the purpose?
  ▷ Even during an emergency?
▷ Validity
  ▷ Is the timing itself the success or are you unwittingly measuring something different, like a manager's ability to gain agreement to an action or everyone's commitment to getting out on time and missing the traffic?

PART
TWO

PART ONE

PART TWO

PART THREE

'd love to say that there is one direct yellow brick road to success where relationships are involved, but that's not been my experience. It's more like a maze with lots of twists and turns, a couple of dead ends, and a few snakes and ladders. We are all such wonderfully complex and unique individuals and every relationship has its own nuances and quirks so that the one-size approach fits absolutely no one.

What that means is that there is no assembly line where you can feed people into a pre-packaged set of workshops at one end and watch them fall off fully wrapped, boxed, and ready to ship back to work at the other.

So rather than giving you a set of rules to follow or boxes to tick, what I want to do is share the thought process that I go through and examples of the tools and techniques that I use, so that you can use them in a way that works for you and your team right now and in the future.

It is called the Dynamic Discovery Journey.

Not everyone starts this journey at the same stage in their life or career, assimilates information at the same speed or in the same way, and not everyone will be ready to hear or benefit from the same messages at the same time because we all have our unique story. But where you and your team are right now doesn't matter in the Dynamic Discovery Journey because it's a path that asks you to open your mind, look on in wonder at those around you, and grow your own brand of wisdom, a way of thinking that just keeps giving.

It is not uncommon for people to attend workshops of this kind more than once in their career and take value from it every time. That's because even though the topic is similar, they are no longer the same person they were the first time around or working with the same team. They come to it with fresh eyes and with different challenges weighing on their mind, or as Heraclitus more beautifully put it, 'No man ever steps in the same river twice. For it's not the same river and he's not the same man.'

To help you navigate it, the Dynamic Discovery Journey is broken down into five steps.

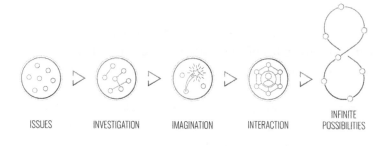

ISSUES   INVESTIGATION   IMAGINATION   INTERACTION   INFINITE POSSIBILITIES

1. Issues
2. Investigation
3. Imagination
4. Interaction
5. Infinite possibilities

They are briefly explained here and then this section takes you through them individually in more detail a chapter at a time.

Step One – Issues

It is always important to begin with exploring your own situation in detail as well as the feelings that are attached to it, along with your ideal outcomes or needs.

Step Two – Investigation

This next step involves identifying the key players and establishing what you know about them and how the context that you are operating in is affecting their relationships and interactions.

Step Three – Imagination

Then it's time to ask 'what if' to give yourself as many options as possible around why something might be happening and how to address it to best serve the needs of individuals or the group.

Step Four – Interaction

Interaction is when you bring the group together. It's implementation, but with a twist, because a Dynamic Discovery workshop is both implementation and ongoing investigation.

Step Five – Infinite possibilities

With the first discovery session completed, you now step aboard the paternoster of infinite possibilities, where you step on and off to meet your needs, blending skill building with deeper exploration and discovery.

The most effective approach is to work through them a step at a time, which is what we will do now.

PART ONE

PART TWO

PART THREE

CHAPTER FIVE

STEP ONE – ISSUES

PART ONE

PART TWO

PART THREE

The process starts with taking stock. It is always important to begin with exploring your situation, the feelings that are attached to it, along with your ideal outcomes, or needs. The subject of working relationships can be both sensitive and overwhelming and it often helps just to get these thoughts and feelings out in the open.

The aim of this initial step is to reflect on and establish quite quickly the level of awareness you have of your current situation and what help is needed.

As with other areas in our lives, sometimes we are unhappy or dissatisfied with our situation but don't know what we need; other times we know exactly what is needed but something else is holding us back.

Here is a selection of situations that teams often find themselves in. One or more of them may apply to you.

▷ A new team just coming together
▷ A group who are a team by name rather than behaviour
▷ Where engagement in the business has been identified as low
▷ A team which struggles with silo behaviour or 'them and us' communication
▷ A group that has undergone a lot of change
▷ Where there are unexpressed tensions that need to be brought to the surface
▷ A group where the behaviour of some is affecting the job satisfaction of others

▷ Where collaboration is necessary but there is resistance
to it

▷ Where it is proving difficult to integrate new people into
an existing team

▷ A team with a legacy of tolerating bad behaviour from
some individuals

▷ Where there is a known conflict, and the group cannot
get past it and move on

▷ A team whose stress levels are high and it's bringing out
the worst in them

▷ Where 'refereeing' between team members is absorbing
excessive management time

We can all be facing similar issues but be at a very different stage
of understanding, accepting, or tackling them, and it's important
to recognise and accept whatever stage you are at and find a
solution that best serves you.

SOMETIMES YOU KNOW

Many leaders know exactly what is needed and just need some
support to take the next step.

Picture the leader who can talk at length about the dynamics
in her team, everyone's history, where the challenges are, why
relationships are strained and what she believes is needed, but
who isn't acting on it.

She has all the necessary knowledge and awareness and a
burning desire to tackle it; the only problem is that the desire to
take on the challenge is as high as the fear of making it worse,
which means that she is turning on the spot.

She feels completely overwhelmed by what she perceives to be a high-risk decision, and worried that if she puts a foot wrong, she'll make it worse and regret it. She needs some reassurance that she is on the right path, a reminder to trust her instincts, and the right support to help her through the discomfort and the process.

Other leaders can see exactly what is going on and are willing to tackle it but lack the skills to act on it.

Of course, you may have the awareness, the skills, and the confidence but suspect that you will encounter resistance. There may be a history of trust issues, or you know you will struggle to be objective given your existing involvement with the team or with some of the team members.

Finally, sometimes you just want to benefit from the development yourself.

SOMETIMES YOU THINK YOU KNOW

It is also possible to start out thinking that you know exactly what is happening and what is needed and then find yourself in this second group. The 'I thought I knew' group. This often shows up like this:

A leader sees the need to pull her team together and is ready to take that on. She experiments with several tried and tested approaches, but for some reason the results are either short-lived or limited to certain people, not including the person causing her the biggest headaches. She is passionate and frustrated in equal measure, putting in considerable amounts of effort for limited reward, and is starting to feel cheated that she isn't getting a fair return on her emotional and practical investment. That leads to questioning her own judgement and her ability as a leader.

If you have ever had a situation in life where you did what you thought was needed and got absolutely nowhere, you can imagine her mounting tension and exasperation.

Like this leader, sometimes we are just too emotionally invested and therefore miss a critical puzzle piece, such as the part that we play in the dynamics of the group we manage. We bring our own story to the way we manage, as you saw in Part One, and sometimes that can be a blind spot for us.

The Parable of the Blind Men and the Elephant illustrates perfectly how we can often be limited by our own view of the world.[41]

The Parable of the Blind Men and the Elephant (simplified)

There was once a group of blind men who were curious about an animal called an elephant.

Being blind, none of them had ever seen one, so they set out to touch an elephant and learn about it that way.

The first man, who touched the trunk of the elephant, said, 'This being is like a thick snake.'

The second man reached for an ear and declared an elephant was like a fan.

The third man who stood by the elephant's leg compared it to a tree.

The man who touched the side of the elephant found it more like a wall.

The man holding the tail described the elephant as being like a rope.

The last felt a tusk and confirmed that the elephant was clearly like a spear, hard and smooth.

When we are standing too close to the elephants in our own lives, we can easily miss what is obvious to those standing further away. The leader I described above wasn't wrong in her interpretation of what was needed, but she was only partly right. To see the whole elephant, or in this case the full picture of why someone was behaving the way they were in her team, she needed to look at it from a different angle.

It can be hard to step back in this way, and often a laser-sharp focus on making progress compounds the problem. My experience of learning to play the piano has taught me that when we put too much pressure on the results we want, it can seriously interfere with our ability to focus on the task at hand and all the moving parts. We are living in a desired future rather than focusing on the tiny but critical steps needed to get there.

Do you need to step back and get a different perspective?

What value might you get from slowing down, stepping back, and asking yourself or others what you may have missed?

SOMETIMES YOU JUST WANT SOMETHING

Having said all of that, you don't need a state of emergency to invest in the quality of the relationships in your team or your business.

Why be reactive when you can be proactive?!

If you are new to leadership and want to create the best possible team, then you don't need to wait for issues to arise before you start investing time and energy into helping the team towards more positive and rewarding interactions.

People often say that employees leave their manager rather than their job, and that might not be how you want things to work in your team. Perhaps you've decided that you want to be the sort of manager that team members are sorry to leave when they head off to their next opportunity, which you encouraged them to pursue.

If you have had bad experiences at work yourself, you may feel strongly that no one should ever experience what you did, and want to set strong foundations from the start.

Maybe you've seen another manager get incredible results by focusing on relationships in the team and you want that for yourself and those you manage or lead.

Maybe you just love learning, and this is your next area of focus.

Maybe you just know intuitively that it's the right thing to do.

It doesn't really matter whether you come to this process from a point of frustration or enthusiasm, clarity or confusion. You'll make progress regardless of where you begin. You just need to begin.

SOMETHING TO PONDER

It is important to spend time exploring your situation: what you are feeling, what you need, and what you want.

▷ If you know what you need or want but are not acting on it, what is holding you back?
  ▷ Fear it will escalate?
  ▷ A loss of confidence?
  ▷ Guilt?
  ▷ No idea where to start?
  ▷ No time or desire to tackle it?
  ▷ Too close to the issue to have real impact?

▷ Not sure if you do fully understand the issues or needs? Ask yourself:
  ▷ Are your efforts short-lived?
  ▷ Does the return not match the effort you're putting in?
  ▷ Does there appear to be a missing piece to your puzzle?
  ▷ Are you starting to question your abilities?

TRY THIS

Put four pieces of paper on the floor as if to mark the compass points (no compass required, just spread them evenly) and put an object in the centre that represents your team.

Stand on the first piece of paper facing towards your team object and ask yourself, what is really going on here and why? Answer yourself intuitively and write down whatever comes to mind first.

Now move to the next sheet of paper and imagine that you are a new employee just joining the business and meeting everyone for the first time. What do you see now?

Now move to the third sheet of paper and imagine that you are standing next to a wise friend or family member whose advice you always value. Now ask them what they see.

Finally, step onto the last sheet of paper and imagine that two years have gone by, and you've moved on from leading this team or even this business. It's now all in the past. You worked out what needed to be done and how to do it.

What did you do? And why?

CHAPTER FIVE: STEP ONE – ISSUES

CHAPTER SIX

STEP TWO – INVESTIGATION

PART ONE

PART TWO

PART THREE

Now that you've established your starting point, you need to put that in context. That means a deep dive into the key players and the environment in which the issues are showing up and to what extent the wider context is creating or contributing to the issues. If you relate to the 'sometimes you know' category, then this stage acts as a final sense check. If you are still in the dark, then this can begin to shine a light on your situation.

It is not always easy to separate cause from effect and often it helps to take time to break the possible causes down. Root causes are often operating at three different levels:

1. Organisation
2. Team
3. Individual

ORGANISATION

It's easy to think of team dynamics as being all about people, but our environment plays a significant role in the way we relate to each other. There's not a lot of road rage on empty country roads, but plenty on busy junctions during the rush hour.

In Chapter Two you considered how a stimulus (the things we experience with our senses) sets off the communication process. The first part of the investigation is about looking for things in the environment that may be stimulating certain behaviours in the team.

Everything that happens in a business has a knock-on effect downstream, even if it appears on the face of it to be unrelated or irrelevant to a particular group of people. The size, age, and ownership of the organisation can all affect the way it is managed and how teams engage with each other.

Change projects, restructuring, new leadership, no leadership, fast growth, downsizing, investing in management development, or culture reviews all come with their own vocabulary, leadership body language, visual clues (like key people disappearing into the end office together), and even the smell of the aftershave of that consultant who always turns up just before a big restructure. I used to work in a business where there was someone not so affectionately referred to as Doctor Death because everyone knew that when he turned up on site, someone was about to leave the organisation.

In the same way that I had an emotional response to the ambulance siren, your team may be vigilant to *that* look on your face, the tension in your voice, or your slightly more assertive handshake with the new CEO. Where one person feels reassured by the new business owner behaving in an overtly paternalistic way, another person may get a sense of foreboding that they can't quite place.

You therefore always need to take an interest in what is going on in the wider organisation, what changes were taking place when the issues began, what is being planned, or what ongoing activities may now be taking their toll. Also never underestimate the power of the grapevine or the slightest changes in routine. Just because you think it's a secret doesn't mean that people didn't work it out long ago and are feeling and behaving accordingly.

An example of the power of context in relationships is well illustrated by this true story.

An employee approached the HR team stating that she was being bullied. She described being on the receiving end of behaviour that was both unwelcome and upsetting and she wanted to leave the established team that she had only recently joined. The organisation she worked in was going through constant change and moving from one restructure to the next with constant looming job losses. Inexperienced managers were often unable to access the support they needed and were mostly left to their own devices whether they had the skills to cope with that or not.

The alleged bully was making it almost impossible for the new team member to learn her job, subtly blocking her access to key contacts by speaking to them first, withholding the product or system knowledge she needed to do her job by being 'just too busy' to explain, and claiming the 'good' parts of the shared workload for herself by arriving early.

The behaviour was making the new employee feel unwelcome and undermining her ability to do her job, but this wasn't because the alleged bully was 'out to get' her new team member or simply a horrible human being. Like many others who find themselves in a similar situation, she was terrified that she would lose her job, had no trust in her manager to support her, and lacked the communication skills and confidence to tackle it any other way.

She was engaging in self-protective behaviours to safeguard her livelihood. It was a reaction to circumstances and a reflection of her inability to cope with those circumstances. It could just as easily have showed up as anxiety or other mental health-related absences. Recognition of the role of context in this scenario allowed compassion and understanding to play a part in the resolution, and the colleagues were supported to resolve it amongst themselves, which they did successfully.

You will recall that in Chapter Four I warned you not to fall too easily into the 'fundamental attribution error' trap, by assuming that someone's actions are more likely to be the result of their personality rather than other factors, like the environment or other things they can't control. If you fall blindly into the fundamental attribution trap in this situation then it's easy to conclude that this 'alleged bully' was just not a very nice person and should just have behaved better, that the 'alleged victim' was weak and needed to learn how to stand up for herself, and that the manager didn't care about his people.

If, however, you take a step back and take context, circumstances, and environment into account then you are more likely to conclude that they are all in some way the victims of the same situation, struggling to navigate their environment. If you've not read the books or seen the films *Lord of the Flies* or *Hunger Games*, they would both give you an interesting insight into the power of context to bring out unexpected behaviours in normal people. It's no excuse for bullying, but bullies only exist in context where it serves them in some way to do it. You cannot of course create environments where there is never any change or uncertainty because that isn't realistic, but you can take steps so that it doesn't pit people against each other.

Over the years I have often heard senior leaders say that if someone was a high performer, they'd be more resilient and learn to manage and deal with change and insecurity. That's easy to say when you've got the power to change the system, but with power comes responsibility and that means taking responsibility for creating an environment that helps people succeed rather than fuelling their fears and then questioning their responses to that fear.

If you want your people to work well together, or you want to work better with others, then these contextual factors are always relevant. You may not always have the power to change things directly, but you can help yourself and others to become aware of and process their responses to them.

TEAM

There may also be factors to consider inside the team itself. Every team has a culture of its own no matter how much effort a business puts into its wider culture. And by culture, I mean 'the way we do things around here'.

Here are some useful questions to ponder:

▷ What is your team culture like – what are the unspoken rules?
▷ Who is setting that culture?
▷ How is it maintained?
▷ Is it changing in any way, for any reason?

I once worked with a team where it was considered normal that if you wanted anything done, you didn't go to the line manager, you went to the managing director's personal assistant. This lady was well liked, diplomatic, kind and could tell you exactly how to present your case so that the leadership would respond to your requests and suggestions favourably. In fact, that PA probably had more influencing power than most of the management team put together.

We often assume that leaders set the culture of a team because their role gives them power and authority. It is likely that people will pay attention to what leaders say, what they focus on, what they reward and how they treat people, but never underestimate the internal networks in a team, the person whose opinion matters most, or the person who quietly and persistently pulls people back in line.

Team culture can be influenced by one or two individuals inside or outside of the team who have no official position of authority but instead hold the collective memory of the team. These influencers often know who to talk to about what and have strong allegiances and friendships in or outside of the group. That is often why teams change dramatically when one person leaves or another arrives.

Just for interest, take out your organisation chart if you have one. Remove the normal reporting lines and redraw the lines based on who interacts with whom on a regular basis. Not all lines are created equal, so make those that are regular, long established or business-critical thicker than the odd minor touch point. You can include everything from internal customers to lunchtime walking companions. You may be surprised what you uncover.

A team can be a lonely place when on paper you look like a unit, but someone feels like an outsider because they are there due to some technicality rather than because these are people who they are likely to be interacting with and feel a sense of belonging with.

If some of your team have stronger connections outside of the group than they do inside the group and are therefore working outside of the boundaries of the team culture, then that might be relevant to why your team doesn't feel like a team or why tensions run high. Equally if one person is holding everything together in the middle then it may look like it is working well but can quickly fall apart as soon as that person falls ill or leaves the group.

There may be more subtle but equally relevant power imbalances relating to qualification, gender, heritage, pay grade, experience, working pattern, disability, and relationships with senior members of the business, to name just a few.

The word 'power' often makes people feel uncomfortable. When we strive to value everyone equally and want to believe that we create an environment that is fair and inclusive, it doesn't sit right that some people have more power than others just because of a characteristic outside of their control, but just because we may not like the idea that it happens, it still does!

If someone knows or strongly believes (whether it's factually correct or not) that for historical, societal, or any other reasons someone else's opinion carries more weight than their own, then they put that person in a position of power. Women returning from maternity leave often believe that their opinion carries less weight now than it did before their leave, one department manager may believe they have less power than their counterparts in other functions because of the pay structure, or those without formal qualifications expect the opinions of those more qualified to override their own.

It doesn't matter if others genuinely see you as equal. If you think they have more power than you do, it will affect what you pay attention to, think, feel, and do, and that can impact the relationship. I noticed this first-hand when I first started work as a graduate. Although I had absolutely no experience of my chosen profession, the fact that I came into the business on a graduate programme with additional training and support meant that I acquired a status and position of privilege that affected the way I was treated by some people.

If you are honest with yourself and notice that you may be perceived as being in a position of power even if you find the idea distasteful and have no desire ever to wield that power, you may need to take steps to be open or vulnerable first to address that imbalance.

Leaders often know about many of the factors that are covered here and view them as 'just the way things are around here' without connecting the dots to how they may be impacting day-to-day interactions. But those dots can make all the difference.

INDIVIDUAL

Last but absolutely not least, there are the individual factors to explore, like suspected or known personal issues or backstories like the ones mentioned in Chapter Three, and any other known or suspected experiences during adulthood that have impacted an individual's perspective of themselves, others, and the world at large.

It is doubtful that there is anyone who cannot recall with total clarity a situation in their past that they found painful and that has affected their behaviour or opinions ever since. This can include an infinite number of events from bereavements and break-ups to bullying accusations, boredom, and being unfairly pulled up on performance.

I vividly recall the day a colleague asked me if she could give me some feedback and did the verbal and emotional equivalent of stabbing me in the chest with a rusty carving knife. The feedback wasn't in any way useful; it was character assassination presented as fact, and to this day the words 'Can I give you feedback?' trigger a strength of feeling in me that I consciously need to manage to make sure that I don't miss something genuinely useful or avoid important information that will support my development.

You may have a story that is lodged in your memory in the same way and even though you may not wish to reopen the wound, it could be beneficial for those you work closely with to know that this might be a trigger for you and to work with you so that it doesn't become a blocker in your relationship.

Of course, even if you are ready to be vulnerable, that doesn't mean that everyone else will openly share their stories, tell you about the toxic culture they left behind elsewhere, or how they have been putting on a brave face every time someone announces good news that they desperately crave for themselves. It is always worth asking yourself what else might lie behind surprising behaviour or a reaction you'd consider excessive in the circumstances.

 ACTIVITY

If you do not yet have a team who share personal information, then useful clues may show up in behaviour instead. What upsets them, angers them, or rallies them to someone else's aid?

▷ Can you pinpoint reactions you see around you that seem exaggerated, unexpected, or out of context?
▷ Is that you being overly alert to it or is that really an unusual reaction?

The investigation step is all about casting the net as wide as possible to give yourself as much information as possible for what might be at the root of the issues that you're facing. It may not be an exact science, but you often find that there is more to your issues than first meets the eye. (Or any of your other senses!)

SOMETHING TO PONDER

▷ No relationship plays out in a vacuum, so you need to consider the environmental factors that affect behaviour.

▷ You can encourage people to behave a certain way, but it's more effective to create an environment that encourages it naturally.

▷ Teams have their own sets of rules, or culture, that isn't always created by the leader. Take the time to get to know yours.

▷ Power imbalances can exist in a team even if we actively encourage equality. It is worth exploring where yours might be.

▷ There will always be things we don't know about those around us, but there are often clues in their behaviour to look out for.

PART ONE

PART TWO

PART THREE

TRY THIS

Disclaimer: I am NOT recommending you do this with a real camera.

Imagine putting a covert camera up in the office and pointing it at your team for a few days. Now imagine showing the footage to someone who doesn't work with you and knows nothing about what you do.

Based on the footage, how would they describe:

▷ How the company is structured and run
▷ How work is allocated and carried out
▷ The way the team communicates
▷ The relationships between the individuals and how they feel about each other

What are they seeing to draw those conclusions?

What do you know that they don't know that might affect the interpretation?

PART ONE

PART TWO

PART THREE

CHAPTER SEVEN

STEP THREE – IMAGINATION

PART ONE

PART TWO

PART THREE

CHAPTER SEVEN: STEP THREE – IMAGINATION

N ow it's time to get creative in your thinking because the imagination step is the 'what if' stage where you start to put the pieces together and let your imagination run wild so that you can maximise your chances of bringing the team together and meeting their needs.

 **ACTIVITY**

A good place to start your thinking is by finishing these sentences in as many ways as possible and then considering which are the most likely endings to prepare for.

▷ She might be doing that because...
▷ He probably thinks...
▷ She may be feeling...
▷ They could be waiting for...
▷ She probably wants me to...
▷ This could be his reaction to...
▷ He needs her to stop...
▷ She secretly wants...
▷ They could be doing that because I...

You can hold this part in your head, scribble it on a flip chart, map it out in Post-it notes or load it into a spreadsheet or project plan, whichever way works best for you. The most important thing is that you have lots of ideas and alternatives as you build a loose rather than a rigid plan of action.

> Once you have explored a wide range of 'what ifs' and 'maybes' you can use that to decide how best to approach your time with the group.

Because you can never be *absolutely* sure about your own level of awareness, the information you have about your team, or the impact various factors are having on them individually or collectively, it is important to remember that you are probably assembling a puzzle with missing pieces. But this imagination stage should naturally guide your thinking about how to handle time with the team with regards to:

1. Setting the tone
2. Choosing your approach
3. Balancing the content

SETTING THE TONE

One of the main considerations is what tone you'll want to strike, whether you want to keep it light and fun to release some tension, or whether you are better served by encouraging deeper discussion.

Light and fun

There is certainly plenty to be said for having some fun together. A good way to do this is by converting a conversation topic into a game, like 'Pin the colour on the leader' or 'How well do we know each other bingo'.

Pin the colour on the leader

This works best if you are working with personality profiles, but it could work just as well if you swap personality types for animals or songs.

This is essentially a perception exercise. Team members who do not know the preferences of their leadership team get together in pairs or threes and agree which colours or characteristics best describe the behaviours that each of the leaders demonstrates at work. They then physically stick a sticker of that colour (or animal or song) on an object that represents that leader, or the actual leader themselves if they're present and willing to be stickered. The leaders then share the output of their actual profile, or the animal or song they most relate to and why.

It's good fun, partly because most of us for some unknown reason like sticking a sticker on something, but more importantly because there are two key rules of the game:

1. You can only use positive statements.
2. No one is asked to justify their stickers – but as they are all positive, they are welcome to do so.

It gives a leader a good indicator of how they are perceived and they in turn can talk about how they relate to the stickers and explain the thinking behind their way of working or communicating.

If that sounds daunting or unrealistic rather than fun, start in a smaller group or even one-to-one first to see what reaction you get.

How well do we know each other bingo

The aim of this game is to populate the spaces on a bingo card with names. Ideally as many different names as possible. You can include anything you like, although if the aim is to have fun, then best choose items that are likely to get a laugh or are light-hearted such as:

▷ Loves to sing in the shower
▷ Has named a plant
▷ Loves pasta
▷ Owns an item of clothing with their name on it
▷ Is on first name terms with their local barista

Fun, playful exercises of this kind can give you the chance to share and get to know each other better with no apparent agenda and can provide answers to questions that people are often hesitant about or have never thought to ask each other about who they are, and what matters to them.

In practice, games often naturally draw out discussion that can lead to increased awareness and connection, but you can also bridge the gaps by encouraging people to expand on their choices or by sharing anything new you learned about them during the game.

Deep and meaningful

Sometimes your what ifs make it very clear that fun isn't the appropriate course of action, and deeper discussion and reflection is what is needed or preferable.

If you are keen to prompt deeper discussion about what matters to people and how they see themselves and others, then consider using a simple question.

Questions you could consider might include:

- ▷ What is more important, being right or being fast?
- ▷ What matters more to you, listening carefully or speaking up?
- ▷ What makes a successful meeting/project/team event?
- ▷ What is the best way to deliver good news/bad news?

The explanations for why people give the answers they give can create some real aha moments that change the way they see each other.

If you are aiming to go deep, it is always worth starting slowly and working your way carefully towards the more challenging questions. Starting easy normalises sharing and sparks curiosity in others before moving on to more vulnerable self-disclosure.

If you do a search for 36 questions to support better connection, you'll find both the research to support why this works and examples you can adapt for the workplace. The key is to find the best solution to get everyone talking and to bring key topics identified in the investigation to the surface in a safe way.

If you are unsure whether to go fun or deep, prepare for a bit of both and be ready to change direction.

CHOOSING YOUR APPROACH

Closely related to tone is the approach you take, whether you are subtle or direct about your intentions and whether you try to bring everyone together in one global activity or split the group.

Direct or subtle

You will need to consider whether it would be better received if you are direct about the purpose of any activities by calling it out as an issue that needs addressing or more subtle, by including an awareness or relationship building or connection activity alongside other items on a longer agenda and edging your way in gently.

The aim is not of course to be dishonest about your intentions, but you need to consider whether advertising working relationships as a topic will shut down rather than encourage willing participation. If an event is presented as tackling an issue it can make those who are already feeling vulnerable more anxious, or it might ramp up the defences of those who anticipate coming under attack.

Not everyone feels comfortable being invited to an event where they anticipate being asked to share what they really think even if they do wish that people knew. In some groups and environments, it's easier on the team if you add in an opportunity for discussing relationships as a kind of warm-up or interval instead of as the main event.

If you anticipate high resistance don't let that put you off, just declare upfront that it's expected in the circumstances and encourage people to offer an alternative perspective in discussions. In fact, flagging early that you expect healthy debate often means you can get to the deeper work faster because it sets the tone for honest and open discussion. Scepticism and cynicism have much less power to influence a discussion if they are invited to attend.

Together or separate

Try not to get too caught up in dreaming up the perfect activity to fit your 'imaginings'. Sometimes it's not the exercise you use but how you use it that makes the difference and gets the result. The same question can be discussed by a team of 10 around a conference table or by splitting off into pairs and then consolidating everyone's thoughts.

In some teams discussing things in pairs encourages meaningful discussion whilst in others it feels too intense. Equally a livelier around-the-table debate may mean that discussion is dominated by some of the group, but it also allows for more sharing of information without putting anyone on the spot. When in doubt give yourself the option of doing both. You could set out to have a group discussion but if that leads to a minute's silence you just split the group and try again.

Even if you know your team well, you can never completely plan for or predict what will happen between individuals on the day and what new or unexpected information may come to light, so it is best to give yourself permission upfront to change your mind on the day when you've seen how the group are interacting.

BALANCING THE CONTENT

It's not just the tone and style you need to consider but also the content you include. You can think of the content as either having collective, interpersonal, or individual value and you need to try and capture all three.

Collective

I use the word collective to refer to anything that everyone can benefit from regardless of their role in the issues or their willingness or ability to engage at a deeper level with others in the room. You could think of it as your comfort blanket or safety net. The collective element forms the foundation or backbone of every workshop or interaction and still adds value in some way even if your plans to get everyone talking fall flat.

Anything collective can be presented in handouts in a book or on a slide deck or, in my case, often on the floor. This might include a story, a case study, a theory, a process, a model, or research evidence. My collective framework of choice is a personality model, but you may have an existing management model that you could use. It needs to be something that can generate debate or discussion and encourage people to share something about themselves.

Some groups are quick to personalise a topic regardless of what it is, debating real examples, sharing personal stories, and discussing how it applies to them. Other groups, especially those more cautious of displaying vulnerability, find comfort in keeping the discussion more theoretical and exploring the pros and cons of a model or concept rather than getting into what they may perceive as *the dangerous territory* of how they feel about what it means to them. Regardless of which way it goes on the day, the collective element is important to provide a framework. If you are taking the more subtle approach, it is critical that this model or theory is one that is immediately relevant to your day-to-day work.

Interpersonal

Although information, models, and theory have their place, the aim is not just to provide information that might *if you're lucky* get people thinking about their relationships, but to actively lead them to engage with each other in a more meaningful way. You need the team to see themselves as a group of individuals embarking on a journey together rather than as spectators sitting side by side gathering information. That's where the interpersonal element comes in, which involves finding ways to create interaction around the information.

You will recall that in Chapter Two you reviewed how the communication process works. The best place to begin with interpersonal work is to encourage the group to explore and share the observable part of this process, the responses they observe in themselves and each other. This focus on behaviour moves you away from theory and closer to reality.

You could opt to use the S.A.F.E.R. communication acronym as your model and then use a simple 'Do and don't' exercise, where everyone needs to choose just one response that they already appreciate from every person in the room. If you think that there is unexpressed bad feeling in the group, for example, this is a good way to get two people to express something positive towards each other without putting them on the spot. This has an added side effect that everyone gets lots of good feedback as well as finding out what others consider important enough to mention.

These conversations, regardless of how they are initiated, are, if managed carefully, incredibly powerful at helping flag up misunderstandings or highlighting new ways of working in future without the need for giving personalised feedback about previous unwelcome but unexpressed behaviours.

Individual

You can plan how you will approach your collective and interpersonal elements but sometimes the most powerful impact happens quietly, sometimes painfully, on the inside, hidden from view, as new information affects the way we see ourselves and those around us.

It may not be the model itself but the question someone else asks that flicks the switch in someone's mind and answers the 'why' question that they didn't even know they were asking themselves. Sometimes you won't even find out it happened, you'll just see that something has changed in the way this person responds to or interacts with someone else.

 ACTIVITY

 ▷ Have you ever had a moment of realisation when a phrase someone used delivered the missing piece in a puzzle you'd been trying to assemble for months or even years?

We all have our own lessons to learn and what might not seem like much of a revelation to you is potentially life changing for someone else. I genuinely believe, having seen it again and again, that we can improve relationships dramatically one small revelation at a time.

As amazing as it would be to create or deliver these eureka moments on demand, it doesn't work quite like that. What you can do however is set the stage and create the opportunities for these moments. If you imagine that there is something that someone needs to hear, then try to find an activity that increases their chances of hearing it, whether that's in a discussion or through a story.

The imagination step might not be visible to others but it's probably the most powerful part of the process.

SOMETHING TO PONDER

▷ The tone that best suits the mood affects how you spend your time as a group – are you in need of or best served by light and fun or deep and meaningful?

▷ Resistance or cynicism isn't always an obstacle; sometimes it is a gift.

▷ Collective work is about value that anyone can benefit from even if they are not ready or wiling to engage in deeper discussion, and includes theories, models, and practical tips.

▷ Interpersonal work is about applying the collective work to reality, and the way that it shows up in your relationships.

▷ Inner work is deeply personal, often hidden, and includes aha moments and revelations that you may never find out have happened for people.

TRY THIS

Ask yourself lots of questions to get your mind whirring with ideas and options.

▷ Is there something you know you all agree on that you could use as a warm-up topic to create a sense of togetherness and alignment?

▷ What topics always get them talking?

▷ Can you tackle this head on or is a subtle approach needed?

▷ Do you expect cynicism and resistance from anyone?

▷ What hasn't worked well in the past?

▷ How could you reframe the cynicism to help you? e.g. thanking people for taking the time to really question and understand. What information would benefit everyone regardless of how much they choose to engage?

▷ What if... you asked the team to share something about themselves that is revealing about who they are but doesn't call for too much vulnerability? e.g. their first job and what it taught them

▷ Are you willing to accept that not all success might be immediately visible to the outside?

▷ What are you hoping some will say or do?

▷ What do you wish someone asked you?

CHAPTER SEVEN: STEP THREE – IMAGINATION

CHAPTER EIGHT

STEP FOUR – INTERACTION

hen it's time to bring the team together and get them interacting with each other. This is implementation but it's implementation with a twist because this interaction is also an ongoing investigation as your time together will give you more pieces to add to your puzzle.

I like to bring groups together in the morning, allowing for conversations to carry over into lunchtime and beyond, embedding the ideas and creating opportunities to agree next steps whilst the ideas are fresh. It's worth taking timing into account and allowing space immediately or soon afterwards for reflection and ongoing discussion.

Whether you are enthusiastic to get started or feeling slightly apprehensive at this stage, the important thing to remember is that this isn't the opening night of a theatre production with you as the lead performer on stage. This is about proactively creating more positive working relationships with those around you, and you are in this to learn and connect and encourage others to do the same.

I suggest you see it as a type of triage system where the aim is to raise awareness, for yourself and for others, and to explore the team dynamics as well as the whys behind the hows of your current communication styles and interactions. The aim of this time together is to facilitate better connection whilst bringing things to the surface that may need further exploration. Everyone, including you, is both investigator and the investigated, sharing and gathering new information about yourselves and each other and revising your perceptions and points of view. Whatever happens, it's useful information.

GETTING STARTED WITH PERCEPTIONS

It's important to ease people in gently, to warm them up to sharing. Research tells us that we are more receptive to learning if we feel physically and psychologically safe[42] and people are more likely to be open to new ways of thinking if they can relax without an expectation of sharing their deepest secrets or exorcising demons from their past.

I often open a first interactive session by bringing some items with me, placing them on the table in front of me and asking, 'Which 2 of these 3 objects that I've put on the table do you think belong to me?' You learn a lot about how they think and what they think of you in this process and can highlight just how fast we make assumptions about people based on how they look or speak, the job they do, or what we've been told about them. If you do this, choose objects that show a side to you they may not know.

There are plenty of other things you could do to get a team to reflect on their perceptions of each other, like the bingo in Chapter Seven, asking everyone to share something interesting that others might not know about them or three work-related facts, where only two are true, and then asking the others to guess which one is false and why. The aim is not to go deep early (although that can happen), but to acclimatise everyone to sharing as much or as little as feels comfortable.

It is often easier to encourage teams to share what they are thinking and feeling if you start by taking about yourself first and take the focus away from them, but this works as a team activity too where everyone brings objects.

INTRODUCING A MODEL OR THEORY

Once you're all warmed up and you've gauged the willingness of those in the room to engage, you can move to the collective element you plan to use.

As I shared in Chapter Four, I normally use a personality profiling tool that translates personality traits into colour as the foundation for this first interaction, and build all interactive activities around that model.

If you are not using this approach, then any model that encourages discussion around different ways of communicating or interacting at work will be useful. There are plenty of models you can refer to which offer different perspectives for discussion. You could use an existing management model, discuss the S.A.F.E.R. acronym from Chapter Two, or even bring a blog about different personality styles and try to work out who relates to which one.

The model or models provide the structure you hang your interactions on as you learn about each other by sharing what you relate to and why. It's good to give an overview of your chosen topic and why you chose it and then get the group interacting around it as quickly as possible.

STYLES AND PREFERENCES IN ACTION

You will have considered at the imagination stage how best to meet the needs of the group and here is where you put that into action.

Ensure you cater to those who are more task orientated, by talking about the impact this model could have on the way you do your work and the results you'll get if you apply it. Then turn that around and discuss the impact the model could have on the way you interact with each other.

Regardless of your own preferences you need to create opportunities to talk and move around to keep them energised and hold their attention, whilst creating opportunities for one-to-one interaction. Never underestimate the power of the break for the talkers to share and the reflectors to slip away quietly for some time and space to think.

If the aim of the interaction is to raise awareness and create positive connection, you need to encourage honesty whilst quickly tackling any comments or behaviour that will shut down honesty from others. That means you need to be a keen observer of people's responses not just verbally but also in their body language. It is incredible how much emotion you can see in someone's eyes if you're open to seeing it.

▷ Just stop and reflect for a moment on the last time you were in a discussion and a challenging situation presented itself. Did the facilitator seize the opportunity to protect everyone's self-esteem?
▷ How do you handle these things?

It is not uncommon in workshops for someone in the room to express a throwaway judgement of a particular approach which triggers emotions for someone else in the room who feels spoken to either directly or indirectly. These situations are blessings in disguise because they create opportunities to put to bed common misconceptions. It's important never to leave a throwaway comment or a strong opinion hanging. If you welcome the comment and offer an alternative perspective, just for balance, it acknowledges the person who said it and the person who didn't want to offer the alternative but feels just as strongly.

Also be aware of the use of humour. 'Many a true word said in jest' is not just another saying. The truth is often wrapped in humour in the hope that it makes it more palatable for others, which it sometimes does but often doesn't. I often respond to those sorts of jokes with a joke that says the opposite. If you are not that fast on your feet, then just stick to acknowledging the use of humour and that they make a valid point and offer up the alternative perspective.

DEALING WITH THE UNEXPECTED

Given the personal nature of this work, and the complexities of human interactions, coming together in this way can generate laughter and lively debate, but it can also highlight deeper issues that need to be addressed either then and there or on another day. You'll need to be prepared for that.

I remember a group I worked with a few years ago who had worked together for a long time and generally got on well. Although there was no expressed conflict or bad feeling in the group, their manager was frustrated, believing that two individuals were holding back in some way, not sharing what they felt. Her view was that this silence was a blocker to the group delivering at their best.

Rather than spending time focusing on searching for issues between individuals we invited the team to have some fun instead using their personality profiles. During the process of exploring how two very different behaviours or approaches can stem from the same intentions, the issue popped up all on its own. These two team members spontaneously declared to each other and the group that they had been misinterpreting each other's behaviours for years and had missed opportunities to collaborate better. That led to some deeply personal sharing which was a key turning point for them individually, the team, and the business.

That sort of aha moment is the norm rather than the exception in these sessions if you are open to it because it is so much easier to acknowledge that we struggle with the behaviours of a specific personality type or style than to look someone in the eye who behaves that way and say we have always found them confusing or even hard work!

It's not always that easy or straightforward of course; sometimes things rise to the surface when you least expect them. I met a team recently with no apparent issues, just a desire to get to know each other better. As the group generally became more animated, the energy in the room picked up and the chat turned to laughter, one person began to fade more and more into the background, turning his focus inwards and away from the group.

As others shared stories about what shaped them, he looked on, realising that the role he played in the team and in life generally wasn't where he wanted to be. For him, as for many others, the incredible accuracy of the individual personality report was both liberating and uncomfortable and he needed time to process that.

A team interaction is not the time or the place to support these individual journeys in depth, but it is the place to spot them and let the person know that it is both normal and safe.

What is important to remember is that these sessions can spark tears of joy and painful realisations, and like Forrest Gump's box of chocolates, you never quite know what you're going to get.

SOMETHING TO PONDER

▷ All interaction is both implementation and investigation. Aim for discovery.

▷ Always warm the team up to sharing with some light or fun discussion. If this is a novel concept for your team, then you may need to ease them into it over a period of time.

▷ Using a personality profiling tool is a great way to talk about different preferences and styles but if you do not have access to that then just debate a blog on the subject instead.

▷ Remember to meet everyone's needs which includes time to talk and time to reflect.

▷ Be ready to offer the alternative to any statement to ensure everyone's views are represented even if they do not voice them directly.

▷ When feelings run deep eureka moments can happen. Trust the process and they will come when they are ready.

TRY THIS

Questions are a powerful tool and here are a few to try.

▷ How can we make sure that we meet everyone's needs?
▷ If we were being more task focused, how would we do it differently?
▷ If we were being more relationship focused, how would we do that differently?
▷ Who else do we need to involve?
▷ What facts are we missing?
▷ What is our agreed next step?
▷ How do we make sure x/y/z feels heard?

CHAPTER EIGHT: STEP FOUR – INTERACTION

CHAPTER NINE

STEP FIVE – INFINITE POSSIBILITIES

CHAPTER NINE: STEP FIVE – INFINITE POSSIBILITIES

With your Dynamic Discovery Journey well underway, you now step aboard the paternoster of infinite possibilities.

If you've not seen one before, a paternoster is a lift that travels on a loop, going up on one side and down the other side of a building rather than just going up and down one lift shaft. There are no doors, just openings, and the lift doesn't stop, it is constantly moving, so you leap off when you reach your destination whilst the lift and anyone in it continues going either up or down. At any time, it is possible to get out, step across, and carry on in the other direction.

As no business, no team, and no person are ever the same, on the same path or tackling the same issues, it is hard to know with any certainty upfront what the next step might be or the path a team will follow, so rather than follow a prescribed set of steps, you just get on and off to suit your needs, whether that is about focusing on skill building or deeper exploration and discovery.

Some people go on to do individual work, whilst others continue to work through a variety of topics together as a team over a period of months.

Depending on the issues you have identified and what came out of your investigation, imagination, and interaction steps, here are some examples of what frequently comes up for others and some ideas that might help you move on further as a team once that first interaction is done.

ADAPTING TO OTHERS

If you've learned a lot about each other and found that liberating and helpful, then most groups start asking:

▷ What practical steps can we take to embed what we've learnt about each other in daily reality?
▷ How do we need to change the way we work to benefit from what we've discovered?
▷ How do we keep up the momentum?
▷ How do we adapt our style to meet x or y's needs in the team?

The answer to all these questions is the same. You need to normalise conversations around relationships and the quality and impact of your interactions. Sharing needs to become the norm rather than the exception.

To do this you also need to become behaviour detectives, which means actively looking for and acting on behaviour clues. In the S.A.F.E.R. communication process in Chapter Two I talked about this process in detail and it's the Stimulus and Response areas that you need to be looking for and talking about with each other.

Lots of teams share with me that weeks after an interaction session around personality they are commenting on the 'redness' of their own approach or saying things like 'That's very blue of you' to each other. The accuracy of the statements is less relevant than the fact that it has become normal and acceptable to notice and comment on behaviour in an observational rather than judgemental way.

Even if you do not opt in to the language of colour, you can still notice that someone's expression changed, that your colleague was quieter than usual in the meeting, more animated around a certain topic, or more focused on the facts than on how everyone was feeling today.

If you are unsure how to normalise this, you can make it an activity at a team meeting for everyone to write down what they've observed, such as: who spoke most, who asked questions, who opened discussion, who shared which facts, who verbally supported another person's ideas with which words or actions, and who attempted to get closure by doing what?

The key is to keep it factual, and non-judgemental, which can be trickier than it sounds. If you are unsure whether you are ready to facilitate this, I suggest you start with the group only giving you feedback on your behaviour so that you can then model adjusting your behaviour as a result.

By adjusting, I mean wherever possible taking into consideration the needs and wants of others. That may be as simple as remembering to ask for someone's opinion rather than expecting them to speak up or creating space in the agenda for discussion rather than quickly moving from one action to the next. Essentially, it's about offering others the stimulus that best serves them to operate at their best, whilst still ensuring that you are not ignoring your own needs.

CONNECTION

Sometimes a first interaction raises awareness of how disconnected a team feels. In this case you may need to carry on with more work around actively creating better connection. In Chapter One you reflected on how you currently rate the level of connection in your relationships. You could take a similar exercise to your team and ask them to do the same.

Why not get everyone individually to score their sense of connection to the team out of 10 using these statements as a guide:

- ▷ The people I work with daily understand me.
- ▷ I can have meaningful rather than just superficial conversations at work.
- ▷ I share interests or ideas with those I work with; we have things in common.
- ▷ They seem to know what I might think or feel about something.
- ▷ I can often predict what others will think or feel about something.
- ▷ Overall, we communicate well.
- ▷ I trust those I work with.
- ▷ I feel comfortable being myself at work.
- ▷ I have a sense of belonging.

Then ask them how they felt about the scoring process without the need to share their answer or the reasons for the answer. If that goes well, and they are comfortable with that, you can move on to sharing one thing that would help move everyone's score up by one point.

You can do this before a meeting, as part of a meeting, or even before and after to gauge the impact of a connection activity.

If that exercise is outside of your comfort zone, or the team is not ready for that depth of sharing, then a simple valuing exercise may be what you need. Get everyone to write down one thing that they value about each person in the room. This doesn't need to be deep and meaningful, it can be as simple as 'I appreciate that you are never late, which is great as I'm so busy' or 'You never forget my birthday; it's nice to be remembered'.

Everyone is then handed their 'What I value about you' statements and the team share what they received and how that feels. Not only does this mean that you are now having meaningful rather than superficial conversation, but you are also telling each other something positive about each other, which supports better connection.

There are plenty of connection-related activities and the key is not to lose sleep looking for exactly the right one, but to get started and try a few to see what works for you.

EXPECTATIONS

If the first interaction highlighted to you that unrealistic expectations were at the root of conflicts in the past, then you may now want to invest some time in understanding and expressing expectations within the team.

Even though we might be good at asking or setting expectations about the content or outputs of a meeting or project, we are not always as good at expressing our expectations when it comes to our relationships and the content or process of communication within them.

 **ACTIVITY**

How certain are you that others fully appreciate how you like to be communicated with:

▷ How sure are you that they know how to disagree with you?
▷ Do they understand your preferred attitude to unsolicited advice?
▷ Would they know when support feels like support to you rather than an intrusion?

As with all exploration, it's easier to start expectation discussions with the lighter, practical topics and then work your way up to the trickier, more vulnerable ones. You could start by taking a few minutes at the start of a meeting or project to ask these sorts of questions:

▷ What is the most important thing to remember when communicating with you?
▷ How will we let each other know if we want or need support?
▷ What does good support look like for you?
▷ How is it best to let you know if I have an issue I want to raise?

It's easy to be disappointed when our colleagues don't meet the expectations we have of them, but what chance do any of us have to get it right if we're not asking and telling each other?

You don't need to promise that suddenly everyone will get all their expectations met but at least if you know each other's

PART ONE

PART TWO

PART THREE

expectations at some level you can start to try or at least manage them.

TRUST

Sometimes there are trust issues in a team that need further attention. These can be due to past mistakes and misunderstandings or because of personal or business insecurities.

Trust touches so many aspects of our relationships and sits right across the entire communication process, so it can be complex to unpick trust issues. It can also be tricky to talk about trust in a team where there isn't much of it, as you don't necessarily trust each other with the truth, and the vulnerability that may come hand in hand with sharing the truth.

The most important thing to remember is that trust is about safety. I trust you if I feel safe around you and expect to keep feeling safe around you, so whatever you do around trust, it needs to feel safe.

Sometimes the best way to do that is to talk about safety rather than trust, or to focus your attention outside of the team by reviewing one of the many trust models available and talking more generally about how to build trust intentionally with clients or suppliers. Often this external focus takes the pressure off sharing whilst still creating a platform to raise awareness of how everyone perceives certain behaviours and why.

TEAM CULTURE

Team culture and how we work collectively is the natural next step for a lot of teams once the focus on understanding everyone individually has started to embed. In the investigation stage you will have considered 'the way we do things in our team', but now is the opportunity to take a closer look not just at how you show up but how you want to, as well as to uncover some of the unspoken rules that you may have missed previously.

I use a variety of exercises to draw that out depending on the needs of the group and whether they are using the language of colour or not. A fun one to try yourself if you want to start the discussion around team culture is to get the group to design an object or machine that represents the team.

They'll need to debate and discuss it and be able to draw, describe, or even build or model its core features, why it needs them, how it's powered, and how it's maintained. You might get a folding broom or a time machine, but what they produce is less relevant than what you glean from the conversation that takes place during the process. This can be even more powerful if you break a bigger team into pairs or threes and compare the results.

You could even go a step further and ask them how the design would change if they asked a key customer, supplier, a peer group, or colleagues from another function.

As you start to talk about 'who we are' and 'how we work' you will begin to draw out where there is a lack of alignment or where the culture isn't serving you, giving you areas to work on.

TEAM EFFECTIVENESS

Some teams want to leap straight into improving their overall effectiveness. They want to know if there is an ideal team mix and what steps, if any, the team can take to design the perfect team. They are often disappointed that there is no ideal mix, but that instead there is an ideal attitude towards adapting your approach, maximising your strengths, and finding ways to manage the gaps.

People often say that there's no 'I' in team, but I believe that a team is all 'I's. It's a collection of individuals who have their own relationships with each other and their own relationship with the goal that they are collectively striving towards. In a small team of four unique individuals, we get six unique relationships that make up the collective 'we' and adding one person in or taking one person away naturally adjusts those relationships. For maximum effectiveness you need to understand the part everyone already does and possibly wants to play in that team.

This means delving more deeply into what everyone individually brings to the team and to ensure that current ways of working do not mean that some strengths are getting a better deal than others at the expense of the whole group or any individual.

I run through a variety of exercises to bring this out, and you can start by asking everyone to write down what they perceive to be their own strengths and where they currently play to them in the team. In the sharing and the discussion that follows you may uncover strengths you didn't know you had or opportunities you've missed. Then you can move on to review how well your day-to-day activities match who is picking them up.

FEEDBACK

You may find that as awareness increases so does the realisation that there is room to fine-tune some of the existing communications skills, and delivering feedback is often at the top of this list.

Because sharing what we think and feel is such a fundamental part of our relationships with others there are lots of feedback models and plenty of books written on the topic. There really is no shortage of advice, and yet much of it focuses on the execution rather than on the quality of relationship that you want at the end of it. As I don't think there is one correct or ideal way of doing most things, I like to share the pros and cons of different models and work through it as a series of considerations.

If feedback is your next area to address, then I suggest you begin by focusing on where it often goes wrong. People often don't fully appreciate WHY they are even giving feedback. There are three main reasons for giving feedback; the first is to meet your needs, the second is to meet someone else's needs, and the third is to develop the relationship, which I'm going to suggest meets both of your needs. So, you need to be clear who it's really for.

Are you genuinely doing it to support their development or are you trying to look like a good manager by encouraging them to change their behaviour to something more compliant or socially acceptable? Are you sure that this is really serving them or are you the one being served by getting it off your chest?

The second issue is around WHO the feedback is aimed at. The giver and the receiver are both relevant to the process (S.A.F.E.R.) and often we try to make it fit for one and not the other. You need to consider what you know about this person and what they've told you about how they like to be communicated with. Are they more likely to want all the facts to support your point or a 'We're in this together' collaborative approach, for example? What do you value and are you overemphasising that?

Only then do you get into the realms of HOW you might actually deliver some feedback for which there are some key ingredients. You'll need some facts. You cannot argue, although *some* will try, with something you can prove in some way. 'You were disrespectful' is interpretation, 'You rolled your eyes upwards' is fact. If there are no facts, whether it's words used or actions taken, you have no foundations, and what you say may fall over as lacking substance.

Feelings are also a key ingredient, and by feelings I don't mean 'I felt like you weren't listening' but actual feelings like being frustrated or angry, disappointed or irritated, confused or surprised.

You also need to connect the dots between the two. For example, you may need to share that when they rolled their eyes it really hurt you, and you interpreted or experienced that as a brush-off, as if your opinion didn't matter.

This is quite a big topic but if you want to get started on your own, I suggest working on spotting your feelings, and separating them from the facts and your interpretation of the two, or go back to Chapter Two and make sure you're not missing anything.

MORE TOPICS TO CONSIDER

This stage is called infinite possibilities because the options really are endless. Other topics you might want or need to explore include stress and managing change, persuading and influencing others effectively, and making compassionate or emotionally intelligent choices.

You could delve into identity and respect and reflect on how your *needs* compare to your *wants* in your relationships, build on your general communication skills, and set some clearer boundaries for yourselves as a team. If it's affecting your relationships and positive relationships are the destination, then whatever rises to the surface needs to find its way onto the agenda.

SOMETHING TO PONDER

▷ There is no right or wrong next step in development, only the one that best serves you at the time.

▷ Are you ready for what is needed next or does there need to be a stepping stone in between?

▷ Do you need to dig deeper, learn more, or apply what you know in practice?

▷ Do you need to do more work in the head or are you ready to do work that leads with the heart?

▷ What revelations are still the topic of conversation - is it worth striking whilst those revelations are still hot?

TRY THIS

If you are unsure where to go next, why not do a collective decision matrix? Imagine that this is topic pick and mix at the sweet shop (only better for your health and happiness). List all the topics that you are keen to explore and then rate them against each other and decide which would serve you more and why.

Example: Topic 1 wins over topic 2 because... topic 2 is of more value than topic 3 because... etc. etc.

Now see what comes out on top. When you are down to the final three, agree between you what to work on next. If you can't agree your next session without things getting ugly, then your next session is on resolving conflict. There you go, solved!

PART ONE

PART TWO

PART THREE

PART
THREE

YVONNE GUÉRINEAU

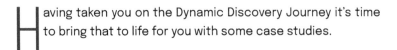

Having taken you on the Dynamic Discovery Journey it's time to bring that to life for you with some case studies.

The examples in these case studies are all taken from teams that I have worked with and are therefore a true-to-life reflection of what I come across on a day-to-day basis. However, to protect the identity of those involved and to give you a wider range of examples to work with I have adapted some of the details and combined scenarios from more than one team or business.

By working through these examples, you'll be able to see how the pieces fit together, the issues the teams faced, how they came out the other side, and how you could get the same results in your business or with your team.

You'll also find some more activities here that you might want to adapt for your own team.

PART ONE

PART TWO

PART THREE

CASE STUDY ONE

MONKEYS GONE BY

YVONNE GUÉRINEAU

CASE STUDY ONE: MONKEYS GONE BY

magine a team where everyone is smiling as they go about their work but is secretly terrified that at any moment a bomb in their midst is about to detonate. That was what was happening in this team.

Putting on a brave face, this group of people were tiptoeing around and tolerating one team member who they believed was the cause of all their upsets and dissatisfaction.

They were unhappy with their situation, but afraid to tackle it in case things got even worse, and therefore trapped and struggling when they really didn't need to be.

ISSUES

This manager came to me in a state of total exasperation, visibly exhausted, weighted down by the burden of a team member who was making everyone's life a misery, including his own. Every time he had a one-to-one with any of his team, the same person was *always* cited as a source of irritation, and he'd had enough.

His team claimed to be tiptoeing around and accommodating this one apparently volatile yet distant individual who appeared to be at best oblivious and at worst indifferent to the discomfort and unhappiness she was causing others.

The manager was between a rock and a hard place because most of his team was unhappy, and threatening to vote with their feet, whilst the source of all the disruption and unhappiness was a hardworking, loyal employee who, although out of step with everyone else around her, was neither underperforming nor doing anything that you'd class as inappropriate.

In fact, she was the most knowledgeable and experienced person in the team, knew the systems inside out, was respected by customers, and got her work done to a high standard. She was just, well, hard to get on with! To the manager it felt like a no-win situation.

He physically shrank in his seat as he shared how he'd tried *everything* he possibly could, over a period of months, making suggestions to the team around how to work with her and encouraging her to integrate herself more into the team, but nothing lasted for long. She didn't see the need and they were fed up with trying.

The attention was now turning on the manager and his ability to lead. The pressure was on him to put things right.

INVESTIGATION

I encouraged the manager to offload his frustrations by asking him a series of questions to unpick what might be going on with the team, the role he played, and why nothing appeared to have worked so far. The deeper I probed, the more the picture began to come into focus.

Organisation

Although the business was well established and profitable with no plans for restructuring or big changes, they had been gradually introducing system changes in the past few years which had had a disproportionately high impact on this team. In theory it was making their lives easier; in practice they were having to change a lot of their long-standing processes to accommodate the system. They were experiencing instability parading as progress.

Team

There were six team members, with the newest team member less than a few months into the job and the longest serving, who also happened to be the lady at the root of the issues, with service in double figures.

The team had unusually high staff turnover for the company and the industry because the new hires rarely stayed for long. Even though no one ever said so directly when they left, it was well known on the company grapevine that people liked the job and the company, they just didn't want to work with 'her'.

Most of the team appeared to be good friends, spending time together socially outside of work.

Individual

Considering how long she'd been there, no one seemed to know anything about the lady at the centre of this drama. No one, the manager included, felt comfortable asking her questions about her life outside of work either. The team had allegedly made plenty of effort in the distant past but as they were generally met with stern looks and curt responses along the lines of 'I've got work to do' they'd gradually all backed away and now communication was primarily by email even though they sat next to each other in a small office.

IMAGINATION

As I was being told about the team dynamics, I kept thinking about the Five Monkey Experiment:

Five Monkey Experiment

Five monkeys were put in a cage.

The cage was bare apart from a ladder leading to some bananas.

The cage was rigged so that every time a monkey climbed to the top of the ladder to reach the bananas an unpleasant spray of icy water was shot at the cage, affecting all the monkeys.

It didn't take long for the monkeys to establish the link between the ladder and the discomfort, so that every time a monkey climbed the ladder the others would pull them down in anger.

Soon the ladder was ignored by all.

The experimenters then replaced one of the monkeys with a newcomer, who, unaware of the water spray, headed up the ladder towards the bananas. No doubt baffled by the angry response from the other monkeys, the monkey soon stopped and integrated into the group.

CASE STUDY ONE: MONKEYS GONE BY

Over time the experimenters replaced one monkey after another until none of the original monkeys remained, and every time the pattern repeated itself.

Soon the cage was full of monkeys avoiding bananas even though none of them had any idea why.

I couldn't help wondering if the person apparently at the source of the problem was actively avoiding the working relationships due to a painful company history that no one else knew about.

I also noticed and pointed out to the manager that he seemed nervous of confrontation and was unsure how to handle someone who appeared to show no sign of emotion when he was clearly very much in touch with his own. When I suggested that I could help draw this out without a big confrontation, his shoulders dropped, and he looked noticeably relieved.

I realised that along with the interpersonal issues between colleagues, this team also had a manager who had lost his confidence and credibility as a leader. It was important for him to be a key part of the solution.

I needed to help them all snap out of it!

I wasn't sure who would do it, but someone needed to take the first step onto the ladder and make a grab for the 'banana', and I had to make sure that they were given that opportunity and that no one held them back.

INTERACTION

I recommended that we bring the group, including the manager, together for a general team get-together to integrate the newest team members and to have some time away from the office together after a busy few months.

They all completed questionnaires for profiles ahead of the day with the intention of using them to get to know each other better and have some fun doing it. There was some resistance initially, but once it was clear that there was no requirement to share their profiles with anyone else, everyone agreed.

I brought a series of warm-up activities that assumed that no one in the group knew anyone else, to give them the opportunity for a complete reset. I also consciously kept things work focused to remove the risk that anyone, especially the lady I expected to be either closed and distant or openly cynical, would feel any pressure to share personal information.

As anticipated, there was some hesitation around the room, but they all participated and when her turn came to share, the lady in question reluctantly shared a few interesting snippets from her long and clearly varied career history. Intrigued by this unknown past, the group initially cautiously and gradually more enthusiastically began to ask her questions about 'the old days' in the company. Faced with genuine interest in her work history, her matter-of-fact tone began to soften a little.

With the room now talking a little more freely I moved on to some fun interactions around styles and preferences and handed out the profiles. That opened the door nicely for me to explain that under high stress or when there is fear of negative consequences, people may not act the way they would otherwise, and to share the monkey story.

The story sparked a discussion about every experience they'd ever had in a 'monkey cage' culture. The concept was easy for everyone in the group to relate to. That was when the lady at the source of the issues piped up and confirmed that, 'Yes, that's how it used to be here, shut up and put up, keep your head down, keep yourself to yourself and get on with your work and you'll be OK.'

The monkey story opened the door, and the rest of the session became increasingly open and honest. The group realised that what they had read as hostility was uncertainty and fear, and felt a new sense of compassion for their alienated team member.

By the end of the event the energy in the room had noticeably shifted and the group left agreeing that they saw each other in a new light.

INFINITE POSSIBILITIES

We could easily have brought this group back together to do deeper work, but they needed time to settle into their new awareness, and the manager needed to take ownership of the situation.

The manager needed a lot of support to understand why he had struggled to confront the issues himself and how his avoidance of conflict had exacerbated the situation, and we did that work one-to-one. He also needed to reflect on his role as the manager of this group and rebuild his confidence.

Whenever I came to the office over the weeks and months that followed, I noticed a definite 'temperature' change in the room and the once silent and stern lady was now noticeably more relaxed and involved in the conversations.

It wasn't an overnight success, because old patterns can be hard to replace, and the manager had a lot of adapting to do, but the staff turnover problem in the team fell away because the people in it were now choosing to stay and work through things together rather than giving up and bailing out.

REFLECTIONS

Not every team has this type of collective breakthrough in their first workshop, but then not every team starts from a point of so much unhappiness and is so desperately in need of this type of breakthrough. In some teams there is one person who naturally steps up and leads the progress and in other teams the change is much more gradual.

It is also worth saying that this manager was willing and able to take responsibility for the role he played in this situation. There are similar scenarios where removing the scapegoat highlights the skill gaps and insecurities of the manager to such a degree that they leave the business shortly afterwards, citing better opportunities. When the aim is to reduce staff turnover and the manager leaves, that may seem counterintuitive, but it is always better to have people who are willing to face or embrace progress or at least accept the support.

CASE STUDY TWO

SETTING SAIL

PART ONE

PART TWO

PART THREE

CASE STUDY TWO: SETTING SAIL

This time imagine a team of 10 where everyone turns up to meetings and contributes what is asked of them, where conversation is polite, where staff turnover is low, and individual performance is high.

Sounds amazing, doesn't it?

Not if you're the manager who has just inherited this team and is run ragged because they are not a team at all, just a group of individuals all on their own path, doing their own thing, expecting you to hold it all together and manage them all individually.

ISSUES

This senior leader was on a mission, announcing in a voice charged with pent-up frustration and utter determination that she *WAS NOT* going to spend the next few months running herself into the ground because her team were used to doing their own thing.

The team she had inherited rarely spoke to each other about their work unless invited to a meeting initiated by her and they expected her to make all their decisions for them. She genuinely believed that their intentions were good and their work ethic high, but they showed no signs of making any effort to pull together as a unit without intervention.

Although she knew what needed to be done in terms of changing the format of meetings, introducing more regular one-to-one time, and changing some of the existing processes, it was all taking longer than she'd expected.

She was getting little feedback or enthusiasm and had hit a brick wall with one senior individual who made all the right noises but then didn't act on it. She was fast becoming disillusioned that the disproportionate amount of mental effort she was already putting into this group wasn't enough.

She wanted and needed help to move things on faster before she lost her cool and did some relationship damage that would be hard to repair.

INVESTIGATION

This leader needed to take a step back and reflect on what she was doing and how she was doing it, what was working, and what wasn't. She also needed to climb out of the trenches and stop trying to do it all single handed to ensure that she reduced her own stress and frustrations. She needed to engage the team more in her efforts so that they were helping rather than hindering her progress.

She struck me as both self-aware and willing to adapt but running on a short fuse. Her expectations were high, and as they were mostly unmet, she was liable to lose her current composure if things didn't improve soon.

Organisation

This was an established owner-managed organisation, that was supportive of its people and generally trusted the teams to get on without excessive supervision or micromanagement. At the same time, it was quite a traditional organisation with established systems and processes, where change had always been slow and considered rather than fast and furious.

Team

The team included some extremely knowledgeable and highly qualified team members as well as others who were equally capable but qualified by experience. Everyone had been there for many years, and they were all loyal and well liked in the business.

There was no obvious antagonism, no heated conversations, and no one complained about each other. The leader suspected that there was something not quite right between two of the group who always chose to sit at opposite ends of a room, but she couldn't quite put her finger on what that was, and the team were not forthcoming with an explanation.

Individual

On an individual level there was little to report, no complex family stories, no health issues, no performance problems, no customer complaints, and no flight risks. Two of the team were around the average retirement age, but neither showed signs of wanting to retire, one because he was needed in the business and allegedly couldn't afford to anyway, the other because she loved the work too much.

The two individuals suspected of the underlying conflict, who tended to keep their distance from each other, were both hard working and, on the surface, appeared happy. There was also a team member referred to as a safe pair of hands and a few showing potential but keeping a low profile.

IMAGINATION

As I was building a picture in my mind of what might be going on here, I was reminded of a duck!

You know the one, floating smoothly across the water whilst underneath the surface the legs are kicking frantically. I was wondering what everyone was thinking underneath the water whilst living the 'polite friendly life' above it. I pondered whether this was partly about style and partly about respect or good manners with some of the team biding their time until two of the team retired, and no one wanting to rock the boat.

For years I had a quote on my wall that said, 'A ship in the harbour is safe but that is not what ships are built for'. This company felt to me like a safe harbour and this new leader wanted more than safety; she wanted to set sail and that was creating waves, with no one else taking up the anchor.

If the team's motivations and intentions were indeed positive, as suspected, then maybe it was all a bit too comfortable and they needed more of a push; alternatively, perhaps some of the group were ready to go, but with so many years of comfortable working just didn't know what to do and how to do it without much clearer and perhaps firmer direction.

I was also asking myself whether the person making all the right noises but not acting on it was nervous of the anticipated changes and unsure how to respond. This might mean that my first impression that the leader was self-aware might not be so accurate and that this was all about her! I needed to get into this team to take a closer look.

INTERACTION

I recommended bringing the group together for a bit of fun and for the leader to get to know them all a bit better. They all completed questionnaires for personality profiles ahead of the day.

I brought a variety of exercises to explore the different perspectives of those in the room in real depth, and there were some 'aha' moments, as well as a few awkward silences, as some of the group realised how frequently their colleagues misinterpreted their intentions and how little they all really knew about each other considering how long they'd all worked there.

I chose to use an activity that draws out the values of different styles and highlights how they are currently being used. This created plenty of discussion and soon some of the team were openly sharing how over time they had adapted to the 'normal' way of working in the business despite it not being their preferred approach.

I encouraged the leader to share her own frustrations about the pace of change and several of the group said they did welcome change but didn't want to be disrespectful to the owners by overtly critiquing the existing ways of working.

At this point it is worth highlighting that these discussions became quite uncomfortable for some of the group, who either became intensely interested in the functional capabilities of their pens or started shifting in their seats. The truth can be very uncomfortable, but sometimes you just need to get through that and out the other side. The way I get around that and help people through it as quickly as possible is to answer the concerns that no one is raising with my own examples.

We worked through some ideas for how the group could approach changes in a way that suited them, and as the session came to an end, I had a strong sense that for a large proportion of the team a weight had been lifted. The others were now in no doubt that their safe harbour of old was open for travel!

I left them in the knowledge that it could take some time to acclimatise and encouraged them to reflect on how best to support themselves and each other through the changes.

INFINITE POSSIBILITIES

I shared my observations with the leader following the session and proposed to give the team some more support to help them navigate and adapt to her new collective working approach.

I used the next workshop to delve further into the skills and preferences of the group and to encourage them to share how they all felt about and responded to change as well as how best to support each other through that. I used a variety of exercises to get them talking about how they like to be treated generally and specifically during tough times.

With the group now much more aware of their collective vulnerabilities and needs we moved on to a third session specifically focused on giving each other feedback. This was quite a big leap for some of the group, who had initially held back their opinions and suggestions, so we took our time over it with a focus on connecting emotionally with the feedback and putting the relationship rather than the process at the centre of the conversation.

It took several months to come through the three workshops and there were a few wobbles in the team along the way, with the person who was making all the right noises at the start struggling to see where he now fit into the wider team or the business and questioning his style and value to the team. I spent time with him one-to-one to help him through that and with the leader helping her to offer the best support.

The two team members who started out sitting at opposite ends of the room also started to work more closely together, having realised that they had more in common than they first thought.

The group came on leaps and bounds as the sessions progressed and the leader now has the mental space to support and develop those who need and want it most more effectively, whilst the group resolve many of their issues with each other without her input.

REFLECTIONS

We never did uncover any serious conflicts or issues in this group; it was just a case of everyone holding back what they were thinking and feeling. This in turn was holding the whole group back. A team doesn't need big problems to benefit from better connection and understanding. The trigger here was the leader who was unwilling to manage a disparate group. In other teams or organisations, maybe even in yours, this is the norm, and no one questions it. It is of course every manager's choice whether they are happy with this arrangement.

It's also worth sharing why this took several months to work through when the leader was already so frustrated. In all honesty, we would not have had the same result if we'd rushed them through it. The group were far too disconnected for there to be anything more than an information transaction in the early days.

The real power for this group, and most groups in my experience, is in the link between the information and the person giving it, who they are, what they really mean, and need and the value this could offer the relationship. I had to work with the leader to create connection first before asking them to take their conversations from head to heart.

Finally, I just want to add that a lot of groups have what I call *wobblers*. There is often someone who needs more time or reassurance, someone who struggles with the vulnerability, or for whom the timing is just unfortunate for one reason or another. I believe that compassion plays a major part in this process, and I do what I can to help, even if that means helping a leader to see that someone just isn't ready. You can create the space and encourage them, but you can't make people want to step into it.

CASE STVDY
THREE

LEADERS AND WARDROBES

YVONNE GUÉRINEAU

Everyone knows that a change is like a holiday. Except of course when it's a change you don't want, which leaves you emotionally battered and bruised and damages your relationships.

This team had experienced the shadow side of change and were struggling to find their way back together afterwards.

I was approached to help them put the pieces back together.

ISSUES

When I met this human resources (HR) leader for the first time, it was like meeting a half-deflated balloon. He seemed to flop in his seat, had bags under his eyes, and looked the subtle shade of green that you'd generally associate with those burning the candle at both ends. He was clearly feeling the strain.

The business, he explained at length, was coming out of a restructuring exercise which had been fast and furious. The leadership team he was a part of were on their knees, and morale in the wider business was low. It had been a punishing few months.

He described how painful it had been for everyone and that as a leadership team they'd struggled emotionally with coming to agreement on some of the staffing decisions they'd had to make. They'd been heartbroken and guilt-ridden watching how people they valued, and who had worked together for years, had said goodbye to friends. They were as shell-shocked as everyone else and putting on a brave face.

Along with the heightened emotions, some very direct and confrontational conversations had taken place within the leadership team in the past months and the air had turned quite a few degrees chillier in their meetings ever since and showed no signs of thawing.

He felt it was his role to support the leadership to reset and recover, but he needed some help to get the ball rolling.

INVESTIGATION

I sensed that there was something else that needed to be said about why he looked quite so battered and bruised by it all. During my time on the frontline of HR I saw my fair share of this type of restructure so I know the toll it can take on people, but at the same time, he was also an experienced HR professional, and I was surprised that this one had hit him so much harder than previous reorganisations.

This felt more personal and to be of real help I needed to know why.

Organisation

He told me the organisation had recently lost a big contract and needed to cut costs fast. They'd restructured to streamline processes, remove inefficiencies, and generally try to do more with less. It was commercially sound but still hard to swallow, because they'd tried their best initially to keep the contract and when that didn't work to bring in work to replace it.

Like so many other organisations in similar circumstances, they'd taken the 'rip the plaster off' approach to get it over quickly and in the hope of making it less painful, but inevitably it had been painful anyway.

Team

There were seven of them in the leadership team and apart from one who had joined nine months previously, they'd all been together for several years.

They had varied backgrounds but mostly in similar industries and prior to the big contract loss they would have described themselves as a good team that communicated well and generally got on.

It was when I probed further into how they all communicated with each other one-to-one that I uncovered that the HR leader and one of the other directors went back years and had been friends long before working together in this business.

Unfortunately, this restructure had created a rift between them. They disagreed on the direction the business was heading, and the HR leader felt cornered as his long-term friend was actively pushing the new agenda and no one else was pushing back even though he knew some of them had reservations.

Individual

I noticed that the HR leader, who spoke confidently about managing conflict around the business, wasn't anywhere near as comfortable discussing his own. He seemed to retreat into himself and chose his words carefully, repeating the phrase 'I know he means well' several times.

The director at the other end of the conflict he described as unafraid to take risks, ambitious, and generally positive in his outlook. He could be hard to speak to when he set his mind on something, regarding anyone who disagreed with him as an obstacle and as being intentionally negative or obstructive.

Apart from the conflict between these two directors there was one other consideration. The newest arrival in the team had slotted in relatively easily but had shown himself to be a bit more direct than they'd expected. In fact, at one point during the restructuring process the sharpness of his tongue had shocked one of the team into silence. Focus on the restructuring meant this had been put on the back-burner where it was now smouldering gently, threatening to reignite at any time.

It was entirely possible that with his feet firmly under the table the newest team member was showing his true colours. Alternatively, of course, this could be purely a stress response to the heightened pressure of joining an established team and stepping straight into a restructuring exercise.

IMAGINATION

This was certainly going to be a tricky one. They all needed some time to recover but they also needed to start talking about what had happened and the impact it had had on them as a group and their relationships.

In the context of trauma, I once heard a therapist describe how unresolved issues are like objects we stuff out of sight into a wardrobe, hoping that the doors will protect us from pain. The wardrobe approach will work for a while, as we stuff more and more inside it, until the wardrobe reaches capacity, the doors fly open, and you get buried under the rubble.

My sense was that this group had been loading the wardrobe and holding the door closed for a while, with the arrival of a new team member and the restructure now pushing their collective wardrobe of repressed conversations to capacity. If I was right, then there was a possibility that things were about to get a lot worse. They needed to open the doors on their own terms, in a safe way, and take a look inside.

What I wanted to know and wasn't clear on just yet was whether this *wardrobe* belonged to a few of the team with the rest of the team mostly unaffected, or whether they were all feeling it equally.

Were some of the team in denial, willing to tolerate it, or genuinely unaffected?

Were some people silently seething and due to blow at any time?

The HR leader wasn't entirely sure himself, so I had to keep our options open.

I was going to have to plan a session for a team that might be cautious and withdrawn but potentially volatile. I had to help them confront the events of the past few months and clear the air whilst helping them feel good about themselves again. There needed to be space to reconnect where there was disconnection and tackle unwanted behaviour that had been left unaddressed.

This had to be less about fun and more about holding the space for the group to gently open the wardrobe doors and look inside.

INTERACTION

Given the size of the group and the time they'd worked together already I recommended an accelerated awareness session moving quickly into the deeper work around communicating during times of change.

I kicked off with a set of exercises to encourage them to remember and share the positives in their relationships and to create space for me to observe their interactions. Although they appeared relaxed, I noticed some caution in the room, with words being chosen carefully. A definite case of walking on eggshells.

I summarised the activities with a focus on how perceptions can change during times of stress because of the way that our focus and often our behaviours change when we are under pressure, and how important it is to look at behaviour in context.

When I took the group through the personal profile part of the awareness session, I put the emphasis on the way in which even the best behaviours can get out of hand under pressure. I chose my examples carefully to make them relatable to their circumstances but generalised enough not to draw attention to any of the existing issues in the room. There were knowing looks around the room as they all reflected on their own behaviour and what they'd seen in others in the past months.

It can be deeply reassuring to discover that how we feel and what we do is perfectly normal, and that was what happened for this group. They were not yet ready to talk openly about how they were feeling but they were asking all the right questions to suggest they were seriously considering it and connecting the dots between their own situation and the examples.

They just needed something to nudge them into talking, so that was the time to bring it closer to reality and share the behaviours I would have expected to see from this group in the past few months based on the preferences that had turned up in their respective profiles. Although I cannot predict behaviour and I don't pretend to know exactly how everyone responds to stress, there are some recurring patterns, and I went through them in turn.

That was when one of the team shared that he recognised some of his behaviour in that description. As one of the quieter members of the team, he went on to share how he'd seen others become more agitated and confrontational, or even frantic, whilst he had become progressively more accommodating, desperate to keep the peace.

There was no great outpouring of feelings, apologies, or critical feedback given that day, but a quiet sense of realisation and acceptance, and some sadness that they had come to this. The 'wardrobe' doors were now open, and I spent the rest of the workshop guiding the group to reflect on the support they all needed from each other now to reset during the tough times still ahead.

This group said their goodbyes looking lighter on their feet, agreeing to come together again soon, and committed to lots of reflection.

INFINITE POSSIBILITIES

This group continued working with me in a variety of ways after the first session.

First, we did a workshop focused on conflict, how they felt about and responded to the conflicts that had arisen between them as a result of the restructure, as well as their collective attitude to risk taking. We worked through several scenarios that the HR leader had agreed with me in advance to ensure they reflected the reality of their working environment and the group agreed specific changes to the way they were working.

Then the two directors who had been friends for many years had some time with me on their own to delve a bit deeper into setting boundaries between home and work so that they could try to reclaim their friendship despite their continued differences at work. My role was not as mediator, but to hold the space, offer structure for their discussions as well as some suggestions.

I also spent some time one-to-one with one of the group who had been relatively quiet throughout and who shared that he was at a junction in his career and personal life. After a few sessions focused on specific actions to take when working with two specific members of the team, we hit on some deeper issues that he needed to address, and he continued that work with a therapist.

With their stress responses and conflict resolution styles now out in the open, we moved on to how they could all improve their approach to giving each other feedback to prevent things escalating to this point in the future. In this workshop there was a great deal of time spent on acknowledging different expectations and styles and how to adapt more effectively to meet each other's needs.

They haven't stopped talking about who they are and how they are with each other, and I have no doubt that they will approach a future restructure very differently.

REFLECTIONS

Although there were no tears or outbursts of any kind in any of my workshops or in the smaller sessions, the team members shared with me independently that they had found the process both emotionally challenging and therapeutic.

This is not uncommon because a lot of this work is by its nature therapeutic. The word therapeutic comes from the Greek *therapeutikos* which means 'to cure or do service, take care of or provide for' and in these sessions the gentle guidance and holding of space allows a group to do that for themselves and for each other. I often find just being in their presence as they do that is also therapeutic for me.

When we are struggling with our relationships it hurts, and what we need is not for anything to be fixed like a broken object, but to heal that relationship or how we feel about it. That sits at the root of what I do, which is why I saved this case study for last.

In this group there was deeper work to do for one of the team and that is not uncommon. As I touched on in Part One, many of us have things in our past that we take with us into work whether we realise it and mean to or not. Sometimes these sessions give people just that little extra incentive or courage to take that step towards deeper work and it is a privilege to be a part of that.

NEXT STEPS

The things that happen to us can change how we see the world and the way we live our lives, often in ways that we can't predict.

If you came to this book in the hope that it might help you improve your relationships at work, then I hope that I have left you in no doubt that relationships are neither a quick fix nor a one-size-fits-all, but a dynamic journey of discovery on the path to putting people in their element.

When you have understood and accepted the deep need that we all have for relationship and connection, begun to appreciate the way we have evolved to get those needs met and the unique way that your life has mapped your own path to achieving it, you'll be on the right path to success.

Although there are theories and processes, techniques, and skills that anyone can learn to improve their interactions, real change isn't something you do on the outside, it's something that happens on the inside.

The most powerful changes in your relationships happen when you make the decision to reconsider your perspective and not just your response. It's when you choose to ask first and act second, to meet someone's needs rather than matching their emotions, and when you take time to see the pain behind the poisonous behaviour.

You now have plenty to be thinking about, but before you put this book away, there are a few final things to say to you.

The first and most important one is that you ALWAYS have a choice! The choice to engage or walk away, to try or not to try, to invest or not to invest in your relationships, or your team. They may not always be attractive choices, easy choices, or obvious choices, but there are always choices, whether you recognise them or not.

The second thing to take away from this book is that there are no guarantees. Even if you choose to invest time and energy in a relationship it doesn't mean it'll work out the way you planned it. That might seem obvious, but it's easily forgotten when you're emotionally invested, desperately want it to work, and are doing your best. People have the right to refuse your efforts, but that doesn't mean they don't appreciate them or want you to stop trying.

Finally, regardless of what you do next, time spent on improving the quality of your relationships is NEVER time wasted. Whatever the outcomes of your attempts, you will always benefit in some way, if only by deepening your understanding of what does and doesn't work for you. You are building a network of connections in your own brain, and one day in the future those connections will be invaluable.

If you have read this far my sense is that working relationships are on your mind, that there is work to do, and that you're ready to do something about it. Maybe you want to talk about the situation you find yourself in, maybe you are ready to bring the team together and flush out the issues, maybe you just want to know more about your options.

My wish for you is that you find exactly what you need to create the relationships you want. You are welcome to try any of the suggestions you've read about here, and I love to hear from people who are on this journey of discovery. You can get in touch on LinkedIn where you will find me at https://www.linkedin.com/in/yvonneguerineau/ or via my website www.yguerineau.com. If I have been of help on your journey, I'd love to hear about it through Amazon reviews too.

If I can be of any more help to you in the future, whether it's a one-off light-hearted away day to bring your team closer together or to explore how best to accompany you and your business on a longer journey of discovery, then please get in touch. I have a contact page on my website or just send me a quick note on LinkedIn.

ACKNOWLEDGEMENTS

A book, like life, is a journey of a million tiny moments. Only a handful of people have had a direct input in the creation of this book and yet it would never have come about if it wasn't for so many people who have been pivotal in my life.

I want to say a special thank you to Xander and Anthony, the two most powerful influencers in my life, for reminding me daily that relationship should and will always be at the centre of everything I do and that who I am and what I do matters in this world.

Long ago I was blessed to meet Christina, who held the space for me to do the work I needed to do on myself to make any of what I do now possible. She holds a special place in my story, and I hope she will take pride in this book as being in some way her achievement too.

I am privileged to have some wonderful friends who have listened tirelessly as I thought out loud to them along the way, who have cheered me on and whose words of support showed me that they believed in this book long before it was written.

I want to thank my clients for trusting me with their businesses, their teams, and their own development. It is a privilege to be part of their journey and they are the daily inspiration to continue with this work.

Thanks also go to Elsa, Caroline, Dom, Rach, Damian, Carrie, John, and Sarah for taking the time to review the manuscript and offer words of support as well as advice on how best to fine-tune my message.

I hope I have done justice to the researchers and authors I have referred to in this book. I have included them because I believe their work matters and I hope I have not misrepresented them in any way.

Finally, I want to thank Karen Williams, The Book Mentor, for her calm and reassuring presence and guidance in this process, Louise Lubke Cuss for her words of wisdom during the editing stage, Sam Pearce of SWATT Books for helping me turn it into an 'actual' book, and to Daniel Moore of Iron Dragon Design for the beautiful models and cover design.

ABOUT YVONNE GUÉRINEAU

Yvonne is a personal growth and deeper connection enthusiast who believes that positive and rewarding working relationships are fundamental to happiness, wellbeing, and success at work and that we all deserve to know how to create them.

She works with business leaders helping them to strengthen interpersonal relationships in their teams so that they can reap the performance and wellbeing rewards that this offers.

Yvonne believes in going deep and getting to the heart of people and their working relationships drawing on her 20 years in human resources, her psychology degree, coaching training, and experience of working with a variety of personality profiling tools to find just the right balance between challenge and support. She encourages individuals to take ownership, lean into discomfort, and experience the personal growth and positive relationships they deserve.

ENDNOTES

1   What does it mean to be human? Smithsonian National Museum of Natural History, https://humanorigins.si.edu/evidence/human-fossils/species/homo-sapiens

2   Feel Better, Live More with Dr Rangan Chatterjee, #89 Why connection is the most important aspect of health: best of 2019, podcast, Podcast Addict, https://podcastaddict.com/episode/91038834

3   Attachment, exploration, and separation: Illustrated by the behavior of one-year-olds in a strange situation, M.D. Ainsworth and S.M. Bell, 1970, *Child Development*, 41:49-67

4   *Harry Harlow: Monkey Love Experiments,* Saul Mcleod PhD, updated 8 February 2023, Simply Psychology, www.simplypsychology.org/harlow-monkey.html

5   Social ties and susceptibility to the common cold, S. Cohen, W.J. Doyle, D.P. Skoner, B.S. Rabin, and J.M. Gwaltney Jr, *Journal of the American Medical Association*, 1997, 25 June, 277(24): 1490-4, https://pubmed.ncbi.nlm.nih.gov/9200634/

6   Social support and health: a review of physiological processes potentially underlying links to disease outcomes, Bert N. Uchino, *Journal of Behavioural Medicine*, 2006 Aug, 29(4): 377-87, https://pubmed.ncbi.nlm.nih.gov/16758315/

7   Social relationships and mortality risk: a meta-analytic review, Julianne Holt-Lunstad, Timothy B. Smith, and J. Bradley Layton, 2010, *PLOS Medicine*, 2010, July 27;7(7), https://pubmed.ncbi.nlm.nih.gov/20668659/

8   Social Relationships and Depression: Ten-Year Follow-Up from a National Representative Study, Alan R. Teo,

HwaJung Choi, and Marcia Valenstein, *PLOS One*, 2013, 8(4): e62396, https://www.ncbi.nlm.nih.gov/pmc/articles/PMC3640036/

9   *Lost Connections - Why you are depressed and what you can do about it*, Johann Hari, 2019, Bloomsbury

10   Can relationships boost longevity and well-being? 1 June 2017, Harvard Health Publishing, https://www.health.harvard.edu/mental-health/can-relationships-boost-longevity-and-well-being

11   Gallup's Employee Engagement Survey: Ask the Right Questions with the Q12 Survey, https://www.gallup.com/workplace/356063/gallup-q12-employee-engagement-survey.aspx

12   A theory of human motivation, A.H. Maslow, 1943, *Psychological Review, 50*(4), 370–396, https://psycnet.apa.org/record/1943-03751-001

13   Self-determination theory and the facilitation of intrinsic motivation, social development, and well-being, R.M. Ryan, and E.L. Deci, 2000, *American Psychologist*, 55(1), 68–78, https://bit.ly/3MMW6cJ

14   *The Gift: 12 Lessons to Save Your Life*, Edith Eger, 2020, Penguin Books, p9

15   *Mindset: Changing the way you think to fulfil your potential*, Dr Carol S. Dweck, revised edition 2017, Robinson

16   Teaching for Learning, Martin M. Broadwell, 20 February 1968, https://www.wordsfitlyspoken.org/gospel_guardian/v20/v20n41p1-3a.html

17   Some Experiments on the Recognition of Speech, with One and with Two Ears (PDF), E.C. Cherry, 1953, *The Journal of the Acoustical Society of America*, 25 (5): 975-79.

18   Unskilled and unaware of it: How difficulties in recognizing one's own incompetence lead to inflated self-assessments, J. Kruger and D. Dunning, 1999, *Journal of Personality and Social Psychology, 77*(6), 1121-1134, https://bit.ly/41EbDQn

19   Confirmation bias, Britannica, https://www.britannica.
      com/science/confirmation-bias

20   *The Body Keeps the Score: Mind, Brain and Body in the
      Transformation of Trauma*, Bessel Van Der Kolk, 2014,
      Penguin Books, p69

21   A Complete Guide to Your Baby's Five Senses,
      verywellfamily, https://www.verywellfamily.com/your-
      baby-senses-smell-touch-taste-sight-hearing-5271010

22   While this quote is commonly attributed to Viktor Frankl,
      its provenance is not clear and it has also been linked
      to Stephen Covey who writes about it in the Foreword to
      *Prisoners of Our Thoughts: Viktor Frankl's Principles for
      Discovering Meaning in Life and Work,* by Alex Pattakos,
      PhD, 2017, Berrett-Koehler Publishers, https://www.
      viktorfrankl.org/assets/pdf/Covey_Intro_to_Pattakos_
      Prisoners.pdf

23   *The Art of Happiness: A handbook for living*, HH Dalai Lama
      & Howard C. Cutler, 1999, Coronet Books, p71

24   Wire together, fire apart: New learning rule aligns
      behavioral and synaptic time scales in place cells, J.
      Krupic, 8 September 2017, *Science*, Vol 357, Issue 6355, pp
      974–975, https://bit.ly/3MO4kBl

25   Quotes by Moshe Feldenkrais, Moving Experience,
      https://www.movingexperience.eu/quotes-by-moshe-
      feldenkrais/

26   John Bowlby Attachment Theory, S. Mcleod PhD, updated 3
      March 2023, *Simply Psychology*, https://simplypsychology.
      org/bowlby.html

27   Attachment Security: Born or Made? J. Belsky, 6 January
      2009, *Psychology Today*, https://www.psychologytoday.
      com/gb/blog/family-affair/200901/attachment-security-
      born-or-made

28   Why Attachment Matters, Children's Services Practice
      Notes, Vol. 19, No. 3, July 2014, https://practicenotes.org/
      v19n3/matters.htm

29 Impact of Neglect on Brain Development and Attachment, Children's Services Practice Notes, Vol. 18, No. 1, January 2013, https://practicenotes.org/v18n1/impact.htm

30 Attachment style quiz, The Attachment Project, https://www.attachmentproject.com/attachment-style-quiz/

31 About the CDC-Kaiser ACE Study, CDC Centers for Disease Control and Prevention, https://www.cdc.gov/violenceprevention/aces/about.html

32 Fast Facts: Preventing Adverse Childhood Experience, CDC Centers for Disease Control and Prevention, https://www.cdc.gov/violenceprevention/aces/fastfact.html

33 The Relation Between Adverse Childhood Experiences and Adult Health: *Turning Gold into Lead*, V.J. Felitti, MD, *The Permanente Journal*, 2002 Winter; 6(1): 44-47, https://www.ncbi.nlm.nih.gov/pmc/articles/PMC6220625/

34 National household survey of adverse childhood experiences and their relationship with resilience to health-harming behaviors in England, M.A. Bellis, K. Hughes, N. Leckenby, C. Perkins, and H. Lowey, 2014, *BMC Medicine*, 12, Article Number: 72 (2014), https://bmcmedicine.biomedcentral.com/articles/10.1186/1741-7015-12-72

35 4 Ways That Adverse Childhood Experiences Affect Adults, 2023, Betterhelp, https://www.betterhelp.com/advice/childhood/4-ways-that-adverse-childhood-experiences-affect-adults/

36 Jean Piaget's Theory and Stages of Cognitive Development, S. Mcleod PhD, updated 8 March 2023, Simply Psychology, https://simplypsychology.org/piaget.html

37 Judgment under Uncertainty: Heuristics and Biases, A. Tversky and D. Kahneman, 1974, *Science*, New Series, Vol 185, No. 4157 (Sep 27, 1974), pp 1124-1131, https://www.science.org/doi/10.1126/science.185.4157.1124

38   How well do you know yourself? Emma Young, 13 October
      2020, British Psychological Society, https://www.bps.org.
      uk/research-digest/how-well-do-you-know-yourself
39   The Fundamental Attribution Error: what it is & how to
      avoid it, Patrick Healy, 8 June 2017, Harvard Business
      School Online, https://bit.ly/41Bfaiz
40   *Jung: A Very Short Introduction*, Anthony Stevens, 1994,
      Oxford University Press
41   Blind men and an elephant, Wikipedia, https://
      en.wikipedia.org/wiki/Blind_men_and_an_elephant
42   Education for Mental Health Toolkit - Psychologically
      safe learning environment, AdvanceHE, https://bit.ly/
      PsychologicalSafetyEd